Hope for All Seasons

Encouragement from *Our Daily Bread*

JULIE ACKERMAN LINK

Discovery House.
from Our Daily Bread Ministries

Requests for permission to quote from this book should be directed to:
Permissions Department, Discovery House,
P.O. Box 3566, Grand Rapids, MI 49501,
or contact us by e-mail at permissionsdept@dhp.org.

All Scripture quotations, unless otherwise indicated, are taken from
The Holy Bible, *New International Version®*, *NIV®*. Copyright © 1973, 1978,
1984, 2011 by Biblica, Inc.® Used by permission of Zondervan.
All rights reserved worldwide. www.zondervan.com.
The "NIV" and "New International Version" are trademarks registered
in the United States Patent and Trademark Office by Biblica, Inc.™

Interior design by Beth Shagene

ISBN: 978-1-62707-652-4

Printed in the United States of America

First printing in 2017

CONTENTS

PART 4: Hope in Beauty and Nature

PART 5: Blessings and Burdens; Challenges and Hope

In the closing paragraph of *Charlotte's Web*, author E. B. White writes: "It is not often that someone comes along who is a true friend and a good writer. Charlotte was both." In my life I can surely say that Julie Ackerman Link was both—"a true friend and a good writer."

I first met Julie in the 1980s when we worked together in the editorial department at Zondervan Publishing House, and for the ensuing thirty-some years we were both professional colleagues and dear friends.

Julie loved words and ideas and creativity. She encouraged writers not only in her role as editor but also through teaching workshops at writers' conferences and in the writing groups she organized and led.

Once Julie saw a purpose in something or in a project, she was determined to see it through. As just one of countless examples, when a friend of hers was going through deep difficulties, Julie determined to encourage her friend by writing specific prayers and devotional thoughts for this person every week for an entire year.

Her purpose and determination were also evident in her disciplined reading through the Bible each year. In doing this, she inspired many of us to do, or attempt to do, the same. And she didn't just read through it superficially to get it done and mark it off her read-through-the-Bible plan. She read deeply and joyfully, and her wise, inspiring, and insightful articles and books grew out of her intense study of the Scriptures.

In 2000, Julie was asked to join the writing staff of *Our Daily Bread* where she became a monthly contributor. Guided by her motto, "Anyone can put words on a page. Only God can breathe life into them," Julie's transparent and honest writing along with her spiritual depth and devotional insight have inspired and challenged millions of lives around the world.

On April 10, 2015, Julie went to be with the Lord she loved and served and wrote about. Now many of her devotionals have been collected in this volume—a spiritual legacy we can enjoy for years to come.

JUDITH E. MARKHAM
former Executive Editor of *Our Daily Bread*
November 2016

PART 1

A Time of Hope

I remember my affliction and my wandering,
*   the bitterness and the gall.*
I well remember them,
*   and my soul is downcast within me.*
Yet this I call to mind
*   and therefore I have hope:*

Because of the LORD's great love we are not consumed,
*   for his compassions never fail.*
They are new every morning;
*   great is your faithfulness.*
I say to myself, "The LORD is my portion;
*   therefore I will wait for him."*

The LORD is good to those whose hope is in him,
*   to the one who seeks him;*
it is good to wait quietly
*   for the salvation of the LORD.*
It is good for a man to bear the yoke
*   while he is young.*

Let him sit alone in silence,
*   for the LORD has laid it on him.*
Let him bury his face in the dust—
*   there may yet be hope.*
Let him offer his cheek to one who would strike him,
*   and let him be filled with disgrace.*

LAMENTATIONS 3:19–30

Though he brings grief, he will show compassion,
so great is his unfailing love. For he does not willingly
bring affliction or grief to anyone.
LAMENTATIONS 3:32-33

It's one of the saddest stories of the Bible, yet it inspired one of the most hopeful hymns of the twentieth century.

The prophet Jeremiah witnessed unimaginable horrors when the Babylonians invaded Jerusalem in 586 BC. Solomon's temple was reduced to ruins, and with it went not only the center of worship but also the heart of the community. The people were left with no food, no rest, no peace, and no leader. But in the midst of suffering and grief, one of their prophets found a reason for hope. "Because of the LORD's great love we are not consumed," wrote Jeremiah, "for his compassions never fail. They are new every morning; great is your faithfulness" (Lamentations 3:22–23).

Jeremiah's hope came from his personal experience of the Lord's faithfulness and from his knowledge of God's promises in the past. Without these, he would have been unable to comfort his people.

This hope of Lamentations 3 is echoed in a hymn by Thomas Chisholm (1866–1960). Although he suffered sickness and setbacks throughout his life, he wrote "Great Is Thy Faithfulness." This song assures us that even in times of great fear, tragic loss, and intense suffering we can find comfort and confidence as we trust in God's great faithfulness.

**The best reason for hope
is God's faithfulness.**

"If you love me, keep my commands. And I will ask the Father, and he will give you another advocate to help you and be with you forever—the Spirit of truth. The world cannot accept him, because it neither sees him nor knows him. But you know him, for he lives with you and will be in you. I will not leave you as orphans; I will come to you. Before long, the world will not see me anymore, but you will see me. Because I live, you also will live. On that day you will realize that I am in my Father, and you are in me, and I am in you. Whoever has my commands and keeps them is the one who loves me. The one who loves me will be loved by my Father, and I too will love them and show myself to them."

Then Judas (not Judas Iscariot) said, "But, Lord, why do you intend to show yourself to us and not to the world?"

Jesus replied, "Anyone who loves me will obey my teaching. My Father will love them, and we will come to them and make our home with them."

JOHN 14:15–23

*Jesus replied, "Anyone who loves me will obey
my teaching. My Father will love them, and we will
come to them and make our home with them."*
JOHN 14:23

As I stood on the Golan Heights, with the Sea of Galilee sparkling in the distance, I listened to our Jewish guide tell about his participation in the 1967 Six-Day War. His vivid accounts of Israel's victories over bigger, more powerful enemies reminded me of Bible stories I learned as a child.

Even though I believe that God has been moving individuals and nations down through history to accomplish His purposes, sometimes I get the idea that God stopped working in people's lives when He finished writing the Bible. Now that He's less visible, I conclude that He's also less involved. But that's not true. Even though God has finished His Book, He hasn't finished telling the story. He's simply using a different form of media to tell it.

In Bible times, God often communicated in tangible, visible, and audible ways—tablets of stone, a pillar of fire, a still small voice, to name a few. But when Jesus came, that changed. He told His followers that God's Spirit would live not only *among* them but also *within* them (John 14:17).

When I long for God to communicate in ways I can see and hear and feel, I need to remember that He is doing something even better. He is living in me, so that through my life the world will be able to see and hear and feel Him.

**God's Spirit lives in us in order
to work through us.**

Sing to the LORD, *all the earth;*
proclaim his salvation day after day.
Declare his glory among the nations,
his marvelous deeds among all peoples.

For great is the LORD *and most worthy of praise;*
he is to be feared above all gods.
For all the gods of the nations are idols,
but the LORD *made the heavens.*
Splendor and majesty are before him;
strength and joy are in his dwelling place.

Ascribe to the LORD, *all you families of nations,*
ascribe to the LORD *glory and strength.*
Ascribe to the LORD *the glory due his name;*
bring an offering and come before him.
Worship the LORD *in the splendor of his holiness.*
Tremble before him, all the earth!
The world is firmly established; it cannot be moved.

Let the heavens rejoice, let the earth be glad;
let them say among the nations, "The LORD *reigns!"*
Let the sea resound, and all that is in it;
let the fields be jubilant, and everything in them!

Let the trees of the forest sing,
let them sing for joy before the LORD,
for he comes to judge the earth.

1 CHRONICLES 16:23–33

Let the heavens rejoice,
let the earth be glad;
let them say among the nations,
"The LORD reigns!"
1 CHRONICLES 16:31

Straight ahead of me, against a clear blue sky on a warm fall day, a small gray cloud was hanging above a busy intersection. I wondered, *What is that lonely cloud doing there on such a perfect afternoon?*

As if hearing my thoughts, the cloud suddenly shimmered like silver and disappeared. Then, just as suddenly, it reappeared, darker this time and in a new shape—a smile. Then I realized the "cloud" was a flock of birds. They stretched across the road like a wavy banner announcing the song that I was hearing on my radio. As the music of "This Is My Father's World" filled my car, the flock of dancing birds seemed to soar with each majestic phrase—dipping with each downbeat and swelling with each crescendo.

I wondered if the other drivers realized that they were in the audience of the Almighty. It seemed to me that all creation was rejoicing in His goodness (1 Chronicles 16:23–33).

With my eyes open, I prayed, "Thank You, heavenly Father, for allowing me to watch. You conduct this remarkable ballet of birds. Thank You for reminding me that all creation, myself included, is part of Your song and that You are conducting every verse. May my praise and worship be as beautiful to You as Your creation is to me. Amen."

All of nature is a grand symphony
conducted by the Creator.

How long, LORD? Will you forget me forever?
How long will you hide your face from me?
How long must I wrestle with my thoughts
and day after day have sorrow in my heart?
How long will my enemy triumph over me?

Look on me and answer, LORD my God.
Give light to my eyes, or I will sleep in death,
and my enemy will say, "I have overcome him,"
and my foes will rejoice when I fall.

But I trust in your unfailing love;
my heart rejoices in your salvation.
I will sing the LORD's praise,
for he has been good to me.

PSALM 13

How long, LORD? Will you forget me forever?
How long will you hide your face from me?
PSALM 13:1

When my husband and I visited Mount Rainier, the fifth highest point in the continental United States (14,411 feet), I expected to see some spectacular sights. But for two days the mountain remained shrouded in clouds. So instead of taking pictures, I bought postcards.

Our vacation caused me to question the way I portray my faith to people around me. Do I present a "postcard" view of Christianity? Do I give the false impression that my life is always sunny—that my view of God is always clear?

That's not what David did. In the passion-filled poetry of Psalm 13, he admitted that he couldn't see God and didn't understand what He was doing (v. 1). But by the end of his prayer, he was certain that what he couldn't see was nevertheless there because he had seen it before in God's bountiful care (vv. 5–6).

Christians are like people living at the foot of Mount Rainier. They've seen the mountain before, so they know it exists even when clouds are covering it.

When suffering or confusion obscures our view of God, we can be honest with others about our doubts. But we can also express our confidence that the Lord is still there by recalling times we've witnessed His grandeur and goodness. That's better than postcard Christianity.

**When living under clouds of adversity,
remember that the sun is still shining.**

A prophecy concerning Nineveh. The book of the vision of Nahum the Elkoshite.

The LORD is a jealous and avenging God;
the LORD takes vengeance and is filled with wrath.
The LORD takes vengeance on his foes
and vents his wrath against his enemies.
The LORD is slow to anger but great in power;
the LORD will not leave the guilty unpunished.
His way is in the whirlwind and the storm,
and clouds are the dust of his feet.
He rebukes the sea and dries it up;
he makes all the rivers run dry.
Bashan and Carmel wither
and the blossoms of Lebanon fade.
The mountains quake before him
and the hills melt away.
The earth trembles at his presence,
the world and all who live in it.
Who can withstand his indignation?
Who can endure his fierce anger?
His wrath is poured out like fire;
the rocks are shattered before him.

The LORD is good,
a refuge in times of trouble.
He cares for those who trust in him,
but with an overwhelming flood
he will make an end of Nineveh;
he will pursue his foes into the realm of darkness.

NAHUM 1:1–8

The LORD is slow to anger but great in power;
the LORD will not leave the guilty unpunished....
The LORD is good, a refuge in times of trouble.
NAHUM 1:3, 7

When we were children, my brother and I recited this prayer every night before supper: "God is great, God is good. Let us thank Him for this food." For years I spoke the words of this prayer without stopping to consider what life would be like if it were not true—if God were not both great and good.

Without His greatness maintaining order in the universe, the galaxies would be a junkyard of banged-up stars and planets. And without His goodness saying "enough" to every evil despot, the earth would be a playground ruled by the biggest bully.

That simple childhood prayer celebrates two profound attributes of God: His transcendence and His immanence. *Transcendence* means that His greatness is beyond our comprehension. *Immanence* describes His nearness to us. The greatness of the almighty God sends us to our knees in humility. But the goodness of God lifts us back to our feet in grateful, jubilant praise. The One who is above everything humbled himself and became one of us (Psalm 135:5; Philippians 2:8).

Thank God that He uses His greatness not to destroy us but to save us and that He uses His goodness not as a reason to reject us but as a way to reach us.

**When you taste God's goodness,
His praise will be on your lips.**

And we know that in all things God works for the good of those who love him, who have been called according to his purpose. For those God foreknew he also predestined to be conformed to the image of his Son, that he might be the firstborn among many brothers and sisters. And those he predestined, he also called; those he called, he also justified; those he justified, he also glorified.

What, then, shall we say in response to these things? He who did not spare his own Son, but gave him up for us all—how will he not also, along with him, graciously give us all things?

ROMANS 8:28–32

He who did not spare his own Son,
but gave him up for us all—how will he not also,
along with him, graciously give us all things?
ROMANS 8:32

A man in Dundee, Scotland who had fallen and broken his back was confined to his bed for forty years. He never had a day without pain, but God gave him the grace and strength to keep going. His cheery disposition and great love for the Lord inspired all who visited him.

One day a friend asked, "Doesn't the devil ever tempt you to doubt God?" "Oh yes, he tries—especially when I have to lie here and see my old schoolmates driving by, having a good time with their families. At times it's as if Satan whispers, 'If the Lord is so good, why does He keep you here? Why did He allow you to break your back?'"

When the friend asked how he handled such attacks, the man replied, "I point him to Calvary and to the wounds of my Savior and say, 'Doesn't He love me!' The devil can't answer that, so he flees every time."

That man's faith in God's love put to rest any doubts about His goodness. He knew that the One who gave His only begotten Son to save him certainly loved him and was working out His good purposes in spite of the accident and all his suffering.

Christian, counter your doubts about the goodness of God by focusing on His sacrificial love.

If you know that God's hand is in everything,
you can leave everything in God's hand.

Praise the LORD.

Praise God in his sanctuary;
praise him in his mighty heavens.
Praise him for his acts of power;
praise him for his surpassing greatness.
Praise him with the sounding of the trumpet,
praise him with the harp and lyre,
praise him with timbrel and dancing,
praise him with the strings and pipe,
praise him with the clash of cymbals,
praise him with resounding cymbals.

Let everything that has breath praise the LORD.

Praise the LORD.

PSALM 150

Praise the LORD.
Praise God in the sanctuary;
praise him in his might heavens.
PSALM 150:1

Psalm 150 is not only a beautiful expression of praise, but it's also a lesson in praising the Lord. It tells us where to praise, why we're to praise, how we're to praise, and who should offer praise.

Where do we praise? In God's "sanctuary" and "mighty heavens" (v. 1). Wherever we are in the world is a proper place to praise the One who created all things.

Why do we praise? First, because of what God does. He performs "acts of power." Second, because of who God is. The psalmist praised Him for His "surpassing greatness" (v. 2). The all-powerful Creator is the Sustainer of the universe.

How should we praise? Loudly. Softly. Soothingly. Enthusiastically. Rhythmically. Boldly. Unexpectedly. Fearlessly. In other words, we can praise God in many ways and on many occasions (vv. 3–5).

Who should praise? "Everything that has breath" (v. 6). Young and old. Rich and poor. Weak and strong. Every living creature. God's will is for everyone to whom He gave the breath of life to use that breath to acknowledge His power and greatness.

Praise is our enthusiastic expression of gratitude to God for reigning in glory forever.

**Praise is the overflow
of a joyful heart.**

"When Israel was a child, I loved him,
    and out of Egypt I called my son.
But the more they were called,
    the more they went away from me.
They sacrificed to the Baals
    and they burned incense to images.
It was I who taught Ephraim to walk,
    taking them by the arms;
but they did not realize
    it was I who healed them.
I led them with cords of human kindness,
    with ties of love.
To them I was like one who lifts
    a little child to the cheek,
    and I bent down to feed them.

"Will they not return to Egypt
    and will not Assyria rule over them
    because they refuse to repent?
A sword will flash in their cities;
    it will devour their false prophets
    and put an end to their plans.
My people are determined to turn from me.
    Even though they call me God Most High,
    I will by no means exalt them."

HOSEA 11:1–7

"How can I give you up, Ephraim?
How can I hand you over, Israel?
How can I treat you like Admah?
How can I make you like Zeboyim?
My heart is changed within me;
all my compassion is aroused."
HOSEA 11:8

The bumper sticker on the blue van caught my attention: "Choose to Feel."

As I considered those words, I noticed the billboards I was passing. They urged me to choose things that would keep me from feeling—alcohol to deaden emotional pain; fat-laden food to alleviate feelings of emptiness; luxury cars and other expensive items to lessen feelings of worthlessness.

Many of the temptations that lure us away from God do so by promising to relieve the emotional hurt we all feel because of the consequences of sin—ours or someone else's.

God set a different example. Instead of becoming numb to the pain our sin causes, He chose to suffer the results of it. Through the prophet Hosea, God expressed the heart-wrenching pain of losing a wayward child. "I bent down to feed them," He said tenderly. "I led them with cords of human kindness, with ties of love" (11:3–4). Still, they rejected their heavenly Father. Reluctantly, He let them face the consequences.

When we choose to feel the full range of our emotions, we come to a fuller understanding of the God who created us in His image—the image of One who feels.

It's okay to feel that all is not right in the world. God feels that way too!

**Choosing to deaden bad feelings
eventually deadens our ability to feel good.**

The LORD, the God of their ancestors, sent word to them through his messengers again and again, because he had pity on his people and on his dwelling place. But they mocked God's messengers, despised his words and scoffed at his prophets until the wrath of the LORD was aroused against his people and there was no remedy. He brought up against them the king of the Babylonians, who killed their young men with the sword in the sanctuary, and did not spare young men or young women, the elderly or the infirm. God gave them all into the hands of Nebuchadnezzar. He carried to Babylon all the articles from the temple of God, both large and small, and the treasures of the LORD's temple and the treasures of the king and his officials. They set fire to God's temple and broke down the wall of Jerusalem; they burned all the palaces and destroyed everything of value there.

He carried into exile to Babylon the remnant, who escaped from the sword, and they became servants to him and his successors until the kingdom of Persia came to power. The land enjoyed its sabbath rests; all the time of its desolation it rested, until the seventy years were completed in fulfillment of the word of the LORD spoken by Jeremiah.

2 CHRONICLES 36:15–21

*"They mocked God's messengers, despised his words
and scoffed at his prophets until the wrath
of the LORD was aroused against his people."*
2 CHRONICLES 36:16

"I love my job," said Maggie, a young nurse, "but it's so frustrating when I tell people what they need to do to stay healthy and they don't follow my advice."

I smiled in empathy. "I felt that way when I started my editorial career," I told her. "It was frustrating when authors would disregard the advice I gave them about improving their manuscripts."

Then I realized the spiritual implication. "If you and I feel frustrated when people don't follow our professional advice," I said, "imagine how God feels when we ignore His." He's the only One with perfect knowledge of what's good for us, yet we often behave as if we know better.

This was the case in ancient Israel. Thinking that they knew more than God did, the people followed their own way (2 Chronicles 36:15–16). As a result, Jerusalem and the house of God fell into the hands of the Babylonians.

This is also the case with us when God's instructions seem difficult. We may conclude that He had exceptions in mind for our particular circumstance.

God graciously teaches what is best (Isaiah 48:17–18) but doesn't force us to do it. He patiently presents what is right and good, and He allows us to choose it.

**God's teaching may not always make sense,
but it's always senseless to think we know better.**

Praise the LORD.

Blessed are those who fear the LORD,
  who find great delight in his commands.

Their children will be mighty in the land;
  the generation of the upright will be blessed.
Wealth and riches are in their houses,
  and their righteousness endures forever.
Even in darkness light dawns for the upright,
  for those who are gracious and compassionate and righteous.
Good will come to those who are generous and lend freely,
  who conduct their affairs with justice.

Surely the righteous will never be shaken;
  they will be remembered forever.
They will have no fear of bad news;
  their hearts are steadfast, trusting in the LORD.
Their hearts are secure, they will have no fear;
  in the end they will look in triumph on their foes.
They have freely scattered their gifts to the poor,
  their righteousness endures forever;
  their horn will be lifted high in honor.

The wicked will see and be vexed,
  they will gnash their teeth and waste away;
  the longings of the wicked will come to nothing.

PSALM 112

Surely the righteous will never be shaken;
they will be remembered forever.
PSALM 112:6

One reason we're left here on earth and not taken to heaven immediately after trusting in Christ for salvation is that God has work for us to do. "Man is immortal," Augustine said, "until his work is done."

The time of our death is not determined by anyone or anything here on earth. That decision is made in the councils of heaven. When we have done all that God has in mind for us to do, then and only then will He take us home—and not one second before. As Paul put it, "Now when David had served God's purpose in his own generation, he fell asleep" (Acts 13:36).

In the meantime, until God takes us home, there's plenty to do. "As long as it is day, we must do the works of him who sent me," Jesus said. "Night is coming, when no one can work" (John 9:4). Night is coming when we will once for all close our eyes on this world, or our Lord will return to take us to be with Him. Each day brings that time a little closer.

As long as we have the light of day, we must work—not to conquer, acquire, accumulate, and retire, but to make visible the invisible Christ by touching people with His love. We can then be confident that our "labor in the Lord is not in vain" (1 Corinthians 15:58).

**In God's eyes,
true greatness is serving others.**

Jesus continued: "There was a man who had two sons. The younger one said to his father, 'Father, give me my share of the estate.' So he divided his property between them.

"Not long after that, the younger son got together all he had, set off for a distant country and there squandered his wealth in wild living....

"When he came to his senses, he said, 'How many of my father's hired servants have food to spare, and here I am starving to death! I will set out and go back to my father....'

"But while he was still a long way off, his father saw him and was filled with compassion for him; he ran to his son, threw his arms around him and kissed him.

"The son said to him, 'Father, I have sinned against heaven and against you. I am no longer worthy to be called your son.'

"But the father said to his servants, 'Quick! Bring the best robe and put it on him. Put a ring on his finger and sandals on his feet. Bring the fattened calf and kill it. Let's have a feast and celebrate. For this son of mine was dead and is alive again; he was lost and is found.' So they began to celebrate.

"Meanwhile, the older son was in the field. When he came near the house, he heard music and dancing. So he called one of the servants and asked him what was going on. 'Your brother has come,' he replied, 'and your father has killed the fattened calf because he has him back safe and sound.'

"The older brother became angry and refused to go in. So his father went out and pleaded with him. But he answered his father, 'Look! All these years I've been slaving for you and never disobeyed your orders.... But when this son of yours who has squandered your property with prostitutes comes home, you kill the fattened calf for him!'

" 'My son,' the father said, 'you are always with me, and everything I have is yours. But we had to celebrate and be glad, because this brother of yours was dead and is alive again; he was lost and is found.' "

LUKE 15:11–13; 17–18; 20–32

All this is from God,
who reconciled us to himself
through Christ and give us
the ministry of reconciliation.
2 CORINTHIANS 5:18

Everybody loves a family story, and today's Bible reading contains one of the most well-known stories in all of Scripture— the Parable of the Lost Son.

Author Henri Nouwen, in his book *The Return of the Prodigal Son*, suggests that all Christians, at some point in their walk of faith, are represented by each of the three main characters. At times we are the wayward child in need of repentance and forgiveness. At other times we are the big brother who wants to hold on to resentment and withhold forgiveness. But as we mature, we become like the father, whose highest desire is to have all his children reconciled.

Nouwen ends the book with these words: "As I look at my own aging hands, I know that they have been given to me to stretch out to all who suffer, to rest upon the shoulders of all who come, and to offer the blessing that emerges from the immensity of God's love."

What role are you playing in your family story? Do you need the courage to repent and seek forgiveness? Or do you need the compassion to extend forgiveness?

God has given His children the "ministry of reconciliation" (2 Corinthians 5:18–19). Would now be a good time to start?

**A right attitude with your family begins
with a right attitude toward God.**

*For I received from the Lord what I also passed on to you:
The Lord Jesus, on the night he was betrayed, took bread, and
when he had given thanks, he broke it and said, "This is my body,
which is for you; do this in remembrance of me."*

1 CORINTHIANS 11:23–24

And when [Jesus] had given thanks,
he broke [the bread] and said, "This is my body,
which is for you; do this in remembrance of me."
1 CORINTHIANS 11:24

When I was growing up, one of the rules in our house was that we weren't allowed to go to bed angry (Ephesians 4:26). All our fights and disagreements had to be resolved. The companion to that rule was this bedtime ritual: Mom and Dad would say to my brother and me, "Good night. I love you." And we would respond, "Good night. I love you too."

The value of this family ritual has recently been impressed on me. As my mother lay in a hospice bed dying of lung cancer, she became less and less responsive. But each night when I left her bedside I would say, "I love you, Mom." And though she could say little else, she would respond, "I love you too." Growing up I had no idea what a gift this ritual would be to me so many years later.

Time and repetition can rob our rituals of meaning. But some are important reminders of vital spiritual truths. First-century believers misused the practice of the Lord's Supper, but the apostle Paul didn't tell them to stop celebrating it. Instead he told them, "Whenever you eat this bread and drink this cup, you proclaim the Lord's death until he comes" (1 Corinthians 11:26).

Rather than give up the ritual, perhaps we need to restore the meaning.

Any ritual can lose meaning,
but that does not make the ritual meaningless.

The priests then brought the ark of the LORD's covenant to its place in the inner sanctuary of the temple, the Most Holy Place, and put it beneath the wings of the cherubim. The cherubim spread their wings over the place of the ark and covered the ark and its carrying poles. These poles were so long that their ends, extending from the ark, could be seen from in front of the inner sanctuary, but not from outside the Holy Place; and they are still there today. There was nothing in the ark except the two tablets that Moses had placed in it at Horeb, where the LORD made a covenant with the Israelites after they came out of Egypt.

The priests then withdrew from the Holy Place. All the priests who were there had consecrated themselves, regardless of their divisions. All the Levites who were musicians—Asaph, Heman, Jeduthun and their sons and relatives—stood on the east side of the altar, dressed in fine linen and playing cymbals, harps and lyres. They were accompanied by 120 priests sounding trumpets. The trumpeters and musicians joined in unison to give praise and thanks to the LORD. Accompanied by trumpets, cymbals and other instruments, the singers raised their voices in praise to the LORD and sang:

"He is good; his love endures forever."

Then the temple of the LORD was filled with the cloud, and the priests could not perform their service because of the cloud, for the glory of the LORD filled the temple of God.

2 CHRONICLES 5:7–14

The trumpeters and musicians joined in unison to give praise and thanks to the LORD. Accompanied by trumpets, cymbals and other instruments, the singers raised their voices in praise to the LORD and sang.

2 CHRONICLES 5:13

Music plays a big part in the Bible. From Genesis to Revelation, God enlists musicians to work on His behalf. He uses music to call people to worship and to send them to war, to soothe ragged emotions and to ignite spiritual passion, to celebrate victories and to mourn losses. Music is an all-occasion, all-inclusive art form. There are followers and leaders, simple songs and complex songs, easy instruments and difficult instruments, melodies and harmonies, fast rhythms and slow rhythms, high notes and low notes.

Music is a wonderful metaphor for the church because everyone participates by doing what he or she does best. We all sing or play different notes at different times, but we all perform the same song. The better we know our parts, and the better we follow the conductor, the more beautiful the music.

One of the best uses for music is praise. When Solomon's temple was completed, the musicians praised and thanked God. As they did, "the glory of the LORD filled the temple of God" (2 Chronicles 5:14).

We thank God for beautiful music because it's like a preview of heaven, where the glory of God will dwell forever and where praise for Him will never cease.

Those who praise God on earth will feel at home in heaven.

He went to Nazareth, where he had been brought up, and on the Sabbath day he went into the synagogue, as was his custom. He stood up to read, and the scroll of the prophet Isaiah was handed to him. Unrolling it, he found the place where it is written:

> *"The Spirit of the Lord is on me,*
>   *because he has anointed me*
>   *to proclaim good news to the poor.*
> *He has sent me to proclaim freedom for the prisoners*
>   *and recovery of sight for the blind,*
> *to set the oppressed free,*
>   *to proclaim the year of the Lord's favor."*

Then he rolled up the scroll, gave it back to the attendant and sat down. The eyes of everyone in the synagogue were fastened on him. He began by saying to them, "Today this scripture is fulfilled in your hearing."

LUKE 4:16–21

He heals the brokenhearted
and binds up their wounds.
PSALM 147:3

Leslie and her two daughters were about to be evicted from their home. Although Leslie believed that God could help, so far He hadn't given a clue as to how. She wondered, *Where is God?* As she drove to the courthouse, she prayed for God's intervention. Then she heard a song on the radio proclaiming, "God is here! Let the brokenhearted rejoice." Could this be the assurance from God that she was longing to hear?

Inside the courtroom, Leslie stood before the judge, heard his decision, and signed the legal documents, but still God had not given her an answer.

As Leslie was walking to her car, a truck pulled up beside her. "Ma'am," said the driver, "I heard your testimony inside the courtroom, and I believe God wants me to help you." And he did. Gary helped Leslie get in contact with a woman from a local church who was able to work with the parties involved to reverse the process so that she and her girls could stay in their home.

When people ask, "Where is God?" the answer is, "Right here." One way God is at work is through Christians like Gary who are continuing the work Jesus started—healing the brokenhearted and binding up their wounds (Psalm 147:3).

**When we love God,
we will serve people.**

David, together with the commanders of the army, set apart some of the sons of Asaph, Heman and Jeduthun for the ministry of prophesying, accompanied by harps, lyres and cymbals. Here is the list of the men who performed this service:

From the sons of Asaph:

Zakkur, Joseph, Nethaniah and Asarelah. The sons of Asaph were under the supervision of Asaph, who prophesied under the king's supervision.

As for Jeduthun, from his sons:

Gedaliah, Zeri, Jeshaiah, Shimei, Hashabiah and Mattithiah, six in all, under the supervision of their father Jeduthun, who prophesied, using the harp in thanking and praising the LORD.

As for Heman, from his sons:

Bukkiah, Mattaniah, Uzziel, Shubael and Jerimoth; Hananiah, Hanani, Eliathah, Giddalti and Romamti-Ezer; Joshbekashah, Mallothi, Hothir and Mahazioth. (All these were sons of Heman the king's seer. They were given him through the promises of God to exalt him. God gave Heman fourteen sons and three daughters.)

All these men were under the supervision of their father for the music of the temple of the LORD, *with cymbals, lyres and harps, for the ministry at the house of God.*

Asaph, Jeduthun and Heman were under the supervision of the king. Along with their relatives—all of them trained and skilled in music for the LORD—*they numbered 288. Young and old alike, teacher as well as student, cast lots for their duties.*

1 CHRONICLES 25:1–8

Kenaniah the head Levite was in charge of the singing;
that was his responsibility because he was skillful at it.
1 CHRONICLES 15:22

When Jason was asked to sing at a church he was visiting, he was delighted to participate even though he wasn't asked until a few minutes before the service started. He chose a familiar hymn, "To God Be the Glory," because it was a song that was especially meaningful to him. He practiced it a few times in the church basement and sang it without accompaniment in the church service.

Several weeks later, Jason learned that some people in the church didn't appreciate his ministry. They thought he was showing off. Because they did not know him, they wrongly assumed that he was singing to impress them, not to honor the Lord.

From the Old Testament we learn that God appointed people with skill to be involved in temple worship. From construction workers to worship leaders, people were chosen based on their skill (1 Chronicles 15:22; 25:1, 7).

The Lord gave each of us different talents and spiritual gifts to be used for His glory (Colossians 3:23–24). When we serve with that purpose, not to lift ourselves up, we don't need to be concerned with what others think. God gave His very best to us—His Son Jesus—and we honor Him by giving our best to Him.

We are at our best when we serve God from our hearts.

Brothers and sisters, I could not address you as people who live by the Spirit but as people who are still worldly—mere infants in Christ. I gave you milk, not solid food, for you were not yet ready for it. Indeed, you are still not ready. You are still worldly. For since there is jealousy and quarreling among you, are you not worldly? Are you not acting like mere humans? For when one says, "I follow Paul," and another, "I follow Apollos," are you not mere human beings?

What, after all, is Apollos? And what is Paul? Only servants, through whom you came to believe—as the Lord has assigned to each his task. I planted the seed, Apollos watered it, but God has been making it grow. So neither the one who plants nor the one who waters is anything, but only God, who makes things grow. The one who plants and the one who waters have one purpose, and they will each be rewarded according to their own labor. For we are co-workers in God's service; you are God's field, God's building.

By the grace God has given me, I laid a foundation as a wise builder, and someone else is building on it. But each one should build with care. For no one can lay any foundation other than the one already laid, which is Jesus Christ. If anyone builds on this foundation using gold, silver, costly stones, wood, hay or straw, their work will be shown for what it is, because the Day will bring it to light. It will be revealed with fire, and the fire will test the quality of each person's work. If what has been built survives, the builder will receive a reward. If it is burned up, the builder will suffer loss but yet will be saved—even though only as one escaping through the flames.

Don't you know that you yourselves are God's temple and that God's Spirit dwells in your midst? If anyone destroys God's temple, God will destroy that person; for God's temple is sacred, and you together are that temple.

1 CORINTHIANS 3:1–17

Do not get drunk on wine, which leads to debauchery.
Instead, be filled with the Spirit, speaking to one another
with psalms, hymns, and songs from the Spirit.
Sing and make music from your heart to the Lord.
EPHESIANS 5:18–19

On a lovely summer evening, a capacity crowd gathered in a beautiful outdoor venue for a concert by one of my college friends. It happened to be his birthday, so the emcee hinted that we might want to sing "Happy Birthday" to him. One by one, people started singing, each in a different key, each at a different tempo. As the jumble of notes and words joined together, the result was, well, less than harmonic. It wasn't even melodious. It was in fact downright pitiful. When my friend took the stage, he gave us another chance. He didn't give us the pitch, but he did give us a downbeat, so at least we were singing together. By the end of the song most people were somewhat close to the same key.

The noise that was supposed to be a song reminded me of a problem in a first-century church. They couldn't agree on their leader. Some followed Paul; others Apollos (1 Corinthians 3:4). The result was conflict and division (v. 3). Instead of music, they were making noise. When people don't agree on a leader, they all "sing" (I'm speaking metaphorically here) at the pace and pitch most comfortable for them.

To make beautiful music that will attract unbelievers to Jesus, all believers must follow the same leader, and that leader must be Christ.

Keeping in tune with Christ
keeps harmony in the church.

As he went along, he saw a man blind from birth. His disciples asked him, "Rabbi, who sinned, this man or his parents, that he was born blind?"

"Neither this man nor his parents sinned," said Jesus, "but this happened so that the works of God might be displayed in him. As long as it is day, we must do the works of him who sent me. Night is coming, when no one can work. While I am in the world, I am the light of the world."

After saying this, he spit on the ground, made some mud with the saliva, and put it on the man's eyes. "Go," he told him, "wash in the Pool of Siloam" (this word means "Sent"). So the man went and washed, and came home seeing.

His neighbors and those who had formerly seen him begging asked, "Isn't this the same man who used to sit and beg?" Some claimed that he was.

Others said, "No, he only looks like him."

But he himself insisted, "I am the man."

"How then were your eyes opened?" they asked.

He replied, "The man they call Jesus made some mud and put it on my eyes. He told me to go to Siloam and wash. So I went and washed, and then I could see."

"Where is this man?" they asked him.

"I don't know," he said.

They brought to the Pharisees the man who had been blind. Now the day on which Jesus had made the mud and opened the man's eyes was a Sabbath. Therefore the Pharisees also asked him how he had received his sight. "He put mud on my eyes," the man replied, "and I washed, and now I see."

Some of the Pharisees said, "This man is not from God, for he does not keep the Sabbath." ...

He replied, "Whether he is a sinner or not, I don't know. One thing I do know. I was blind but now I see!"

JOHN 9:1–16; 25

Once you were alienated from God
and were enemies in your minds because
of your evil behavior.
COLOSSIANS 1:21

For those of us who don't have the spiritual gift of evangelism, the word *witness* can stir up some unpleasant memories or paralyzing anxieties. In fact, I've sometimes felt like a complete failure when I tried to follow methods that were designed to make witnessing easier.

Jim Henderson, author of *Evangelism Without Additives: What if Sharing Your Faith Meant Just Being Yourself*, has made the subject less threatening for me by suggesting another way of thinking about witnessing. Instead of using someone else's words or story, he suggests "just being yourself."

In courtrooms, secondhand testimony is not allowed because anything other than a firsthand account is unreliable. The same is true spiritually. The authentic story of the work Christ has done in our lives is the best testimony we have. We don't need to doctor it or dramatize it. When we tell the truth about Christ's power to save us and keep us from sin, our testimony will be credible.

If the thought of taking classes or memorizing plans has kept you from witnessing, try a different approach: be yourself! Like the blind man Jesus healed, simply say, "I was blind but now I see" (John 9:25).

If you want others to know
what Christ can do for them,
tell them what He has done for you.

PART 2

Life and Hope

When Jesus had finished saying these things, he left Galilee and went into the region of Judea to the other side of the Jordan. Large crowds followed him, and he healed them there.

Some Pharisees came to him to test him. They asked, "Is it lawful for a man to divorce his wife for any and every reason?"

"Haven't you read," he replied, "that at the beginning the Creator 'made them male and female,' and said, 'For this reason a man will leave his father and mother and be united to his wife, and the two will become one flesh'? So they are no longer two, but one flesh. Therefore what God has joined together, let no one separate."

"Why then," they asked, "did Moses command that a man give his wife a certificate of divorce and send her away?"

Jesus replied, "Moses permitted you to divorce your wives because your hearts were hard. But it was not this way from the beginning."

MATTHEW 19:1–8

So the LORD God banished him
from the Garden of Eden to work the ground
from which he had been taken.
GENESIS 3:23

When Pastor Howard Sugden performed the wedding ceremony for my husband and me, he emphasized that we were participating in a miracle. We believed him, but we didn't comprehend the size of the miracle needed to hold two people together, much less become one.

After about twenty years, I realized that the marriage, not the wedding, was the real miracle. Anyone can have a wedding, but only God can create a marriage.

One definition of *wed* is "to cause to adhere devotedly or stubbornly." For some couples, "stubborn" is a more accurate description of their relationship than "devoted."

God has in mind something much better for us than a stubborn refusal to divorce. The union of marriage is so strong that we become "one flesh." God wants marriage to be the way it was when He first created Eve from Adam (Genesis 2:21–24). That's what Jesus was explaining to the Pharisees when they asked Him, "Is it lawful for a man to divorce his wife for any and every reason?" (Matthew 19:3). Jesus replied, "A man will ... be united to his wife, and the two will become one flesh" (v. 5).

To pledge your life to another is indeed an act of faith that requires belief in miracles. Thankfully, God is in the business of creating marriages.

**A happy marriage is a union
of two good forgivers.**

Do we not all have one Father? Did not one God create us? Why do we profane the covenant of our ancestors by being unfaithful to one another?

Judah has been unfaithful. A detestable thing has been committed in Israel and in Jerusalem: Judah has desecrated the sanctuary the LORD *loves by marrying women who worship a foreign god. As for the man who does this, whoever he may be, may the* LORD *remove him from the tents of Jacob—even though he brings an offering to the* LORD *Almighty.*

Another thing you do: You flood the LORD's *altar with tears. You weep and wail because he no longer looks with favor on your offerings or accepts them with pleasure from your hands. You ask, "Why?" It is because the* LORD *is the witness between you and the wife of your youth. You have been unfaithful to her, though she is your partner, the wife of your marriage covenant.*

Has not the one God made you? You belong to him in body and spirit. And what does the one God seek? Godly offspring. So be on your guard, and do not be unfaithful to the wife of your youth.

"The man who hates and divorces his wife," says the LORD, *the God of Israel, "does violence to the one he should protect," says the* LORD *Almighty.*

So be on your guard, and do not be unfaithful.

MALACHI 2:10–16

Has not the one God made you? You belong to him
in body and spirit. And what does the one God seek?
Godly offspring. So be on your guard,
and do not be unfaithful to the wife of your youth.
MALACHI 2:15

The drama played out in a nest of bald eagles monitored by a webcam. A beloved eagle family, viewed by many via the Internet, was breaking up. After raising several offspring in previous seasons, the parents again laid new eggs in the spring. But then a young female invaded their happy home. When Dad started cavorting with her, Mom disappeared and the life in the abandoned eggs died.

In an Internet chat room, questions and accusations flew wildly. Everyone who loved the pair was distraught. Biologists warned the amateur eagle enthusiasts not to attribute human values to birds. But everyone did. We all wanted the original couple to reunite. Everyone seemed to "know" that the family unit is sacred.

As chat room members expressed their sadness, I wondered if they knew that God feels much the same way about human family breakups. I also wondered about myself: Why did I feel more sadness over the eagles than over the fractured human families in my community? Clearly, I need to revise my priorities.

In Malachi 2, we see God's view of marriage. It symbolizes His covenant with His people (v. 11). He takes it very seriously— and so should we.

Put Christ first
if you want your marriage to last.

"My prayer is not for them alone. I pray also for those who will believe in me through their message, that all of them may be one, Father, just as you are in me and I am in you. May they also be in us so that the world may believe that you have sent me. I have given them the glory that you gave me, that they may be one as we are one—I in them and you in me—so that they may be brought to complete unity. Then the world will know that you sent me and have loved them even as you have loved me.

"Father, I want those you have given me to be with me where I am, and to see my glory, the glory you have given me because you loved me before the creation of the world.

"Righteous Father, though the world does not know you, I know you, and they know that you have sent me. I have made you known to them, and will continue to make you known in order that the love you have for me may be in them and that I myself may be in them."

JOHN 17:20–26

I and the Father are one.
JOHN 10:30

My husband is a "numbers" person; I am a "word" person. When my incompetence with numbers gets the best of me, I try to boost my ego by reminding Jay that word people are superior because Jesus called himself the Word, not the Number.

Instead of trying to defend himself, Jay just smiles and goes on about his business, which consists of much more important things than my silly arguments.

Since Jay will not defend himself, I feel compelled to do so. Although I am right about Jesus being the Word, I am wrong in saying that He didn't refer to himself as a number. One of the most moving passages of Scripture is Christ's prayer just before His arrest and crucifixion. Facing death, Jesus prayed not only for himself but also for His disciples and for us. His most urgent request on our behalf involved a number: "[I pray] all of them may be one, Father, just as you are in me and I am in you. May they also be in us so that the world may believe that you have sent me" (John 17:21).

As people who live by the Word, we need to remember that "right words" sound hollow to the world unless we, being one in Christ, are glorifying God with one mind and one voice.

God calls His children to unity.

Dear friends, let us love one another, for love comes from God. Everyone who loves has been born of God and knows God. Whoever does not love does not know God, because God is love. This is how God showed his love among us: He sent his one and only Son into the world that we might live through him. This is love: not that we loved God, but that he loved us and sent his Son as an atoning sacrifice for our sins.

Dear friends, since God so loved us, we also ought to love one another. No one has ever seen God; but if we love one another, God lives in us and his love is made complete in us.

This is how we know that we live in him and he in us: He has given us of his Spirit.

And we have seen and testify that the Father has sent his Son to be the Savior of the world. If anyone acknowledges that Jesus is the Son of God, God lives in them and they in God. And so we know and rely on the love God has for us.

God is love. Whoever lives in love lives in God, and God in them. This is how love is made complete among us so that we will have confidence on the day of judgment: In this world we are like Jesus. There is no fear in love. But perfect love drives out fear, because fear has to do with punishment. The one who fears is not made perfect in love.

We love because he first loved us. Whoever claims to love God yet hates a brother or sister is a liar. For whoever does not love their brother and sister, whom they have seen, cannot love God, whom they have not seen. And he has given us this command: Anyone who loves God must also love their brother and sister.

1 JOHN 4:7–21

The LORD appeared to us in the past, saying:
"I have loved you with an everlasting love;
I have drawn you with unfailing kindness."
JEREMIAH 31:3

What happened between my husband and a dog named Maggie was not love at first sight. In fact, their first meeting was more like a war dance. When Jay came home from work, Maggie stopped him at the back door and growled at him as if he were an intruder. Then Jay growled, wanting to know why a strange dog was in his home. I explained why I rescued her from the kennel, but he was unmoved.

But soon Maggie began welcoming Jay home in the evening with a wildly excited dance routine. With all twenty toenails tapping on the tile she would wag her tail and wiggle to tell him that his arrival was the highlight of her day. Within a week, her enthusiastic welcome had won his heart.

Maggie's method of winning Jay's affection reminded me of what the prophet Jeremiah and the apostle John wrote. God's love for us, they said, draws us into a loving relationship with Him (Jeremiah 31:3; 1 John 4:7–8, 19).

When I think about God enjoying my presence as much as Maggie enjoys Jay's, I am eager to spend time with Him. I realize that God loves me far more than Maggie loves Jay, and my heart fills up with love for Him. And then my heart overflows with love for others, for the power of God's love empowers me to love even those who don't love me.

**We love because
God first loved us.**

"As the Father has loved me, so have I loved you. Now remain in my love. If you keep my commands, you will remain in my love, just as I have kept my Father's commands and remain in his love. I have told you this so that my joy may be in you and that your joy may be complete. My command is this: Love each other as I have loved you. Greater love has no one than this: to lay down one's life for one's friends. You are my friends if you do what I command. I no longer call you servants, because a servant does not know his master's business. Instead, I have called you friends, for everything that I learned from my Father I have made known to you. You did not choose me, but I chose you and appointed you so that you might go and bear fruit—fruit that will last—and so that whatever you ask in my name the Father will give you. This is my command: Love each other."

JOHN 15:9–17

You make known to me the path of life;
you will fill me with joy in your presence,
with eternal pleasures at your right hand.
PSALM 16:11

Maggie doesn't care much for television. She would rather look out a window than stare at a small screen. Reading doesn't thrill her either. She has been known to "chew" on books, but only in the strictly literal sense. Nevertheless, when Jay and I read or watch TV, Maggie participates. Even though she doesn't enjoy what we're doing, she enjoys being with us. Maggie is our very devoted dog. More than anything (well, just about anything) Maggie wants to be with us.

The word *dogged* means "determined and persistent." These words describe Maggie. They should also describe us. When we are devoted to God, we want to be with Him even when He's doing something that makes no sense to us. We may ask, "Why, Lord?" when He seems angry (Psalm 88:14) or when He seems to be napping (44:23) or when the wicked prosper (Jeremiah 12:1). But when we remain devoted to God despite our questions, we find fullness of joy in His presence (Psalm 16:11).

Jesus knew we would have questions. To prepare us for them, He urged us to abide in His love (John 15:9–10). Even when God's ways are inexplicable, His love is reliable. So we remain doggedly devoted to Him.

We find joy when we learn
to abide in Jesus's love.

"Very truly I tell you Pharisees, anyone who does not enter the sheep pen by the gate, but climbs in by some other way, is a thief and a robber. The one who enters by the gate is the shepherd of the sheep. The gatekeeper opens the gate for him, and the sheep listen to his voice. He calls his own sheep by name and leads them out. When he has brought out all his own, he goes on ahead of them, and his sheep follow him because they know his voice. But they will never follow a stranger; in fact, they will run away from him because they do not recognize a stranger's voice." Jesus used this figure of speech, but the Pharisees did not understand what he was telling them.

Therefore Jesus said again, "Very truly I tell you, I am the gate for the sheep. All who have come before me are thieves and robbers, but the sheep have not listened to them. I am the gate; whoever enters through me will be saved. They will come in and go out, and find pasture. The thief comes only to steal and kill and destroy; I have come that they may have life, and have it to the full."

JOHN 10:1–10

I am the gate; whoever enters through me will be saved.
They will come in and go out, and find pasture.
JOHN 10:9

My husband, Jay, and I have a new family member—a two-month-old tabby cat named Jasper. To keep our new kitten safe, we've had to break some old habits, like leaving doors open. But one thing remains a challenge: the open stairway. Cats like to climb. Even as kittens, they know that the world looks better when you're looking down on it. So whenever I have Jasper downstairs with me, she is determined to go upstairs. Trying to keep her confined to a safe place near me has tested my ingenuity. Gates that work with children and dogs do not work with cats.

My cat gate dilemma brings to mind the metaphor Jesus used to describe himself: "I am the gate for the sheep," He said (John 10:7). Middle Eastern sheepfolds were enclosures with an opening for the sheep to go in and out. At night, when the sheep were safely inside, the shepherd would lie in the opening so that neither sheep nor predators could get past him.

Although I want to keep Jasper safe, I am not willing to make myself the gate. I have other things to do. But that's what Jesus Christ does for us. He places himself between us and our enemy, the devil, to protect us from spiritual harm.

**The closer to the Shepherd,
the farther from the wolf.**

As the crowds increased, Jesus said, "This is a wicked generation. It asks for a sign, but none will be given it except the sign of Jonah. For as Jonah was a sign to the Ninevites, so also will the Son of Man be to this generation. The Queen of the South will rise at the judgment with the people of this generation and condemn them, for she came from the ends of the earth to listen to Solomon's wisdom; and now something greater than Solomon is here. The men of Nineveh will stand up at the judgment with this generation and condemn it, for they repented at the preaching of Jonah; and now something greater than Jonah is here.

"No one lights a lamp and puts it in a place where it will be hidden, or under a bowl. Instead they put it on its stand, so that those who come in may see the light. Your eye is the lamp of your body. When your eyes are healthy, your whole body also is full of light. But when they are unhealthy, your body also is full of darkness. See to it, then, that the light within you is not darkness. Therefore, if your whole body is full of light, and no part of it dark, it will be just as full of light as when a lamp shines its light on you."

LUKE 11:29–36

For as Jonah was a sign to the Ninevites,
so also will the Son of Man be to this generation.
LUKE 11:30

The road was smooth and we were making good progress as we headed for Jay's dad's house in South Carolina. As we drove through the mountains in Tennessee, I began seeing detour signs. But Jay kept going, so I assumed that they didn't apply to us. Shortly before we reached the North Carolina border, we came to a sign that said the highway ahead was closed due to a rockslide. We would have to turn around. Jay was surprised. "Why wasn't there any warning?" he wanted to know. "There were lots of warnings," I said. "Didn't you see the signs?" "No," he said. "Why didn't you mention them?" "I assumed that you saw them," I answered. We now tell this story to entertain our friends.

Throughout history, God provided plenty of "signs" to show people the way to live, but they kept going their own way. When God finally sent His Son as a sign (Luke 11:30), the religious leaders paid little attention to His warnings. Life for them was good. They were recognized and respected (v. 43). They resented being told that they were wrong (v. 45).

We can be the same way. When life is going well, we tend to ignore warnings that we need to turn around and change our sinful ways. It's important to remember that we may be wrong even though life is good.

God sends warnings to protect us,
not to punish us.

On another day the angel came to present themselves before the LORD, *and Satan also came with them to present himself before him. And the* LORD *said to Satan, "Where have you come from?"*

Satan answered the LORD, *"From roaming throughout the earth, going back and forth on it."*

Then the LORD *said to Satan, "Have you considered my servant Job? There is no one on earth like him; he is blameless and upright, a man who fears God and shuns evil. And he still maintains his integrity, though you incited me against him to ruin him without any reason."*

"Skin for skin!" Satan replied. "A man will give all he has for his own life. But now stretch out your hand and strike his flesh and bones, and he will surely curse you to your face."

The LORD *said to Satan, "Very well, then, he is in your hands; but you must spare his life."*

So Satan went out from the presence of the LORD *and afflicted Job with painful sores from the soles of his feet to the crown of his head. Then Job took a piece of broken pottery and scraped himself with it as he sat among the ashes.*

His wife said to him, "Are you still maintaining your integrity? Curse God and die!"

He replied, "You are talking like a foolish woman. Shall we accept good from God, and not trouble?"

In all this, Job did not sin in what he said.

JOB 2:1–10

Then the LORD said to Satan,
"Have you considered my servant Job?
There is no one on earth like him;
he is blameless and upright,
a man who fears God and shuns evil."
JOB 1:8

After my father injured his eye so severely that it had to be surgically removed, doctors and nurses commented on how well he accepted the loss. His response was indeed exceptional. Throughout the ordeal I never heard him complain.

After the accident someone asked, "Why would God allow this to happen? What does your dad have to learn at his age?"

Not every tragedy is the result of our being enrolled in God's school of hard knocks against our will. There is always something we can learn from suffering. But in this case, my father was the teacher as well as the student.

Dad's response to pain and loss, combined with my mother's ongoing godly response to her own health problems, is teaching me the lesson that God's servant Job knew was true. At the height of his suffering, his wife urged him to "curse God and die!" (Job 2:9). But Job responded, "Shall we accept good from God, and not trouble?" (v. 10).

Job didn't understand the reason for his suffering, yet he affirmed his steadfast belief in a God who had the right to allow trouble in our lives as well as good. In times of suffering, it's important to consider what God would have us teach as well as what He would have us learn.

Difficulties tend to call out great qualities.

What shall we say, then? Shall we go on sinning so that grace may increase? By no means! We are those who have died to sin; how can we live in it any longer? Or don't you know that all of us who were baptized into Christ Jesus were baptized into his death? We were therefore buried with him through baptism into death in order that, just as Christ was raised from the dead through the glory of the Father, we too may live a new life.

For if we have been united with him in a death like his, we will certainly also be united with him in a resurrection like his. For we know that our old self was crucified with him so that the body ruled by sin might be done away with, that we should no longer be slaves to sin—because anyone who has died has been set free from sin.

Now if we died with Christ, we believe that we will also live with him. For we know that since Christ was raised from the dead, he cannot die again; death no longer has mastery over him. The death he died, he died to sin once for all; but the life he lives, he lives to God.

In the same way, count yourselves dead to sin but alive to God in Christ Jesus.

ROMANS 6:1–11

We were therefore buried with him through baptism
into death in order that, just as Christ was raised
from the dead through the glory of the Father,
we too may live a new life.
ROMANS 6:4

After my doctor announced that I had cancer, I tried to listen to what he said, but I couldn't. I went home, pulled a blanket over my head, and fell asleep on the couch, as if sleeping could change the diagnosis.

When I finally gained enough strength to tell my loved ones, my friend Judy Schreur said something especially memorable. After expressing her sympathy, she said, "This is what will happen. You will feel really bad for three days. Then you will get up, figure out what you have to do, and get on with your life." Then she added, "I think it has to do with death, burial, and resurrection."

At the time, I didn't believe it. I was sure that life as I knew it was over. Nothing would ever be the same. I couldn't imagine feeling normal again. But she was right. Three days later I woke up and realized I didn't feel quite so bad. And little by little, despite the physical misery of chemotherapy treatments, my emotional and spiritual condition improved significantly. I "died" to my old reality and was "raised" to a new normal.

Thankfully, God is in the business of resurrection. For those who have died in Christ, the death of one reality means resurrection to a new, glorious normal so we can "live a new life" (Romans 6:4).

To be "in Christ" is to share in His life,
in His death, and in His resurrection.

Then I saw "a new heaven and a new earth," for the first heaven and the first earth had passed away, and there was no longer any sea. I saw the Holy City, the new Jerusalem, coming down out of heaven from God, prepared as a bride beautifully dressed for her husband. And I heard a loud voice from the throne saying, "Look! God's dwelling place is now among the people, and he will dwell with them. They will be his people, and God himself will be with them and be their God. 'He will wipe every tear from their eyes. There will be no more death' or mourning or crying or pain, for the old order of things has passed away."

He who was seated on the throne said, "I am making everything new!" Then he said, "Write this down, for these words are trustworthy and true."

REVELATION 21:1–5

"There will be no more death or
mourning or crying or pain,
for the old order of things has passed away."
REVELATION 21:4

"Think about how good it will feel when it stops hurting," said my father. I received this advice from Dad often while I was growing up, usually after some minor bump or scrape had resulted in a major dramatic reaction. At the time, the advice didn't help. I was incapable of focusing on anything other than my pain, and loud wails accompanied by buckets of tears seemed the only appropriate response.

Through the years, however, Dad's advice has pulled me through some truly miserable situations. Whether it was the pain of a broken heart or the misery of a drawn-out illness, I would remind myself: Now is not forever.

The confidence we have as Christians is that God has something good planned for us. Suffering was not part of His original act of creation, but it serves as a temporary reminder of what happens in a world where God's order has been broken. It also motivates us to spread the word about God's plan to redeem the world from the suffering caused by sin.

Although we cannot avoid pain and disappointment (John 16:33), we know that it's only temporary. Some sorrow will be relieved in this life, but all of it will be relieved when God finally and firmly establishes His new heaven and new earth (Revelation 21:1). Now is not forever.

**The gains of heaven will more than compensate
for the losses of earth.**

Carry each other's burdens, and in this way you will fulfill the law of Christ. If anyone thinks they are something when they are not, they deceive themselves. Each one should test their own actions. Then they can take pride in themselves alone, without comparing themselves to someone else, for each one should carry their own load. Nevertheless, the one who receives instruction in the word should share all good things with their instructor.

Do not be deceived: God cannot be mocked. A man reaps what he sows. Whoever sows to please their flesh, from the flesh will reap destruction; whoever sows to please the Spirit, from the Spirit will reap eternal life. Let us not become weary in doing good, for at the proper time we will reap a harvest if we do not give up. Therefore, as we have opportunity, let us do good to all people, especially to those who belong to the family of believers.

GALATIANS 6:2–10

Carry each other's burdens,
and in this way you will fulfill
the law of Christ.
GALATIANS 6:2

When I learned I needed chemotherapy, my biggest fear was losing my hair. I knew this was a vain thought and should have been a minor concern, but I rationalized that it was okay to grieve what the Bible calls a woman's glory (1 Corinthians 11:15).

I knew, however, that the loss I was grieving was not my glory but my identity. My hair, which reached to my knees, was so much a part of who I was that I was afraid of losing myself when I lost it. In the past I'd had nightmares about having my hair cut. What would happen when it was really gone? I feared the worst.

But the worst never happened. I had my hair cut short—a little anxiety but no nightmares. And then it fell out—some sadness, but no despondency.

Several weeks later my dear friend Marge said to me, "Julie, I can't tell you how often I have grieved the loss of your hair. It's so much a part of you."

Suddenly I realized that Marge was fulfilling the command of Galatians 6:2: "Carry each other's burdens." She was coming alongside me with prayers and empathy to ease my burden.

Satan wants to defeat us with heavy burdens, but fellow believers by their love and support can minimize the suffering he causes.

Bearing one another's burdens
helps make the burdens bearable.

Then the LORD *God formed a man from the dust of the ground and breathed into his nostrils the breath of life, and the man became a living being.*

Now the LORD *God had planted a garden in the east, in Eden; and there he put the man he had formed. The* LORD *God made all kinds of trees grow out of the ground—trees that were pleasing to the eye and good for food. In the middle of the garden were the tree of life and the tree of the knowledge of good and evil.*

A river watering the garden flowed from Eden; from there it was separated into four headwaters. The name of the first is the Pishon; it winds through the entire land of Havilah, where there is gold. (The gold of that land is good; aromatic resin and onyx are also there.) The name of the second river is the Gihon; it winds through the entire land of Cush. The name of the third river is the Tigris; it runs along the east side of Ashur. And the fourth river is the Euphrates.

The LORD *God took the man and put him in the Garden of Eden to work it and take care of it.*

GENESIS 2:7–15

*"If you listen carefully to the LORD your God and do
what is right in his eyes, if you pay attention to his
commands and keep all his decrees, I will not bring on
you any of the diseases I brought on the Egyptians."*
EXODUS 15:26

The doctors I know are smart, hardworking, and compassionate. They have relieved my suffering on many occasions, and I am grateful for their expertise in diagnosing illnesses, prescribing medication, setting broken bones, and stitching up wounds. But this does not mean that I place my faith in physicians rather than in God.

For reasons known only to God, He appointed humans to be His partners in the work of caring for creation (Genesis 2:15), and doctors are among them. Doctors study medical science and learn how God designed the body. They use this knowledge to help restore us to a healthy condition. But the only reason doctors can do anything to make us better is that God created us with the ability to heal. Surgeons would be useless if incisions didn't heal.

Scientists can learn how God created our bodies to function, and they devise therapies to help restore or cure us, but they are not healers; God is (Exodus 15:26). Doctors simply cooperate with God's original intent and design.

So I am grateful for science and doctors, but my praise and thanksgiving go to God, who designed an orderly universe and who created us with minds that can discover how it works. I believe, therefore, that all healing is divine because no healing takes place apart from God.

**When you think of all that's good,
give thanks to God.**

Your word, LORD, is eternal;
it stands firm in the heavens.
Your faithfulness continues through all
generations;
you established the earth, and it endures.
Your laws endure to this day,
for all things serve you.
If your law had not been my delight,
I would have perished in my affliction.
I will never forget your precepts,
for by them you have preserved my life.

Save me, for I am yours;
I have sought out your precepts.
The wicked are waiting to destroy me,
but I will ponder your statutes.
To all perfection I see a limit,
but your commands are boundless.

PSALM 119:89–96

Your faithfulness continues through all generations;
you established the earth, and it endures.
PSALM 119:90

Jim and Carol Cymbala prayed and praised and preached their way through a personal two-year nightmare. Their teenage daughter Chrissy had turned her back on the God they loved and served so faithfully. Although their hearts were breaking, Jim and Carol continued ministering to the people of the Brooklyn Tabernacle in New York City.

Some people think Carol wrote the song "He's Been Faithful" after her daughter's dramatic return to God, but she didn't. She wrote it before. Carol refers to it as "a song of hope born in the midst of my pain." While hurting deeply, Carol said that her song "became like a balm to my heart, strengthening me once again." The words she wrote during that time helped her to move forward. Although her daughter had not yet come back to the Lord, Carol could praise Him for His loving faithfulness in her own life.

Later, when Chrissy showed up at home and fell to her knees begging forgiveness, the truth of Psalm 119:90 became real to Carol: God is faithful not just to our generation, but to all generations! Carol also experienced in a new way a line of her own song that has blessed so many: "What I thought was impossible, I've seen my God do!"

When we have nothing left but God,
we find that God is enough.

Praise be to the God and Father of our Lord Jesus Christ! In his great mercy he has given us new birth into a living hope through the resurrection of Jesus Christ from the dead, and into an inheritance that can never perish, spoil or fade. This inheritance is kept in heaven for you, who through faith are shielded by God's power until the coming of the salvation that is ready to be revealed in the last time. In all this you greatly rejoice, though now for a little while you may have had to suffer grief in all kinds of trials. These have come so that the proven genuineness of your faith—of greater worth than gold, which perishes even though refined by fire—may result in praise, glory and honor when Jesus Christ is revealed. Though you have not seen him, you love him; and even though you do not see him now, you believe in him and are filled with an inexpressible and glorious joy, for you are receiving the end result of your faith, the salvation of your souls.

1 PETER 1:3–9

In all this you greatly rejoice,
though now for a little while you may have
had to suffer grief in all kinds of trials.
1 PETER 1:6

When I opened my Bible to read Jeremiah 1 through 4, the subhead ascribed to the book startled me: "Hope in Time of Weeping." I almost cried. The timing was perfect, as I was walking through a season of weeping over the death of my mom.

I felt much the same way after hearing my pastor's sermon the day before. The title was "Joy in Suffering," taken from 1 Peter 1:3–9. He gave us an illustration from his own life: the one-year anniversary of his father's death. The sermon was meaningful for many, but for me it was a gift from God. These and other events were indications backed up by His Word that God would not leave me alone in my grief.

Even though the way of sorrow is hard, God sends reminders of His enduring presence. To the Israelites expelled from the Promised Land due to disobedience, God made His presence known by sending prophets like Jeremiah to offer them hope—hope for reconciliation through repentance. And to those He leads through times of testing, He shows His presence through a community of believers who "love one another deeply, from the heart" (1 Peter 1:22). These indications of God's presence during trials on earth affirm God's promise of the living hope awaiting us at the resurrection.

We need never be ashamed of our tears.
—DICKENS

So Boaz took Ruth and she became his wife. When he made love to her, the LORD enabled her to conceive, and she gave birth to a son. The women said to Naomi: "Praise be to the LORD, who this day has not left you without a guardian-redeemer. May he become famous throughout Israel! He will renew your life and sustain you in your old age. For your daughter-in-law, who loves you and who is better to you than seven sons, has given him birth."

Then Naomi took the child in her arms and cared for him. The women living there said, "Naomi has a son!" And they named him Obed. He was the father of Jesse, the father of David.

This, then, is the family line of Perez:
Perez was the father of Hezron,
Hezron the father of Ram,
Ram the father of Amminadab,
Amminadab the father of Nahshon,
Nahshon the father of Salmon,
Salmon the father of Boaz,
Boaz the father of Obed,
Obed the father of Jesse,
and Jesse the father of David.

RUTH 4:13–22

The women said to Naomi:
"Praise be to the LORD, who this day has not
left you without a guardian-redeemer."
RUTH 4:14

A wise person once told me, "Never be quick to judge whether something is a blessing or a curse." The story of Naomi reminds me of this.

The name *Naomi* means "my delight." But when bad things happened to her, Naomi wanted to change her name to match her circumstances. After her husband and sons died, Naomi concluded, "The LORD's hand has turned against me!" (Ruth 1:13). When people greeted her, she said, "Don't call me Naomi.... Call me Mara, because the Almighty has made my life very bitter" (v. 20).

Rather than judge her circumstances in light of her identity as a follower of the one true God who had proclaimed unfailing love for His people, Naomi did what most of us tend to do: She judged God in light of her circumstances. And she judged wrongly. The hand of the Lord had not gone out against her. In fact, Naomi had a God-given treasure she had not yet discovered. Although Naomi lost her husband and two sons, she was given something totally unexpected—a devoted daughter-in-law and a grandchild who would be in the lineage of the Messiah.

As Naomi's life shows us, sometimes the worst thing that happens to us can open the door for the best that God has to give us.

God's purpose for today's events
may not be seen till tomorrow.

"Ah, Sovereign LORD, you have made the heavens and the earth by your great power and outstretched arm. Nothing is too hard for you. You show love to thousands but bring the punishment for the parents' sins into the laps of their children after them. Great and mighty God, whose name is the LORD Almighty, great are your purposes and mighty are your deeds. Your eyes are open to the ways of all mankind; you reward each person according to their conduct and as their deeds deserve. You performed signs and wonders in Egypt and have continued them to this day, in Israel and among all mankind, and have gained the renown that is still yours. You brought your people Israel out of Egypt with signs and wonders, by a mighty hand and an outstretched arm and with great terror. You gave them this land you had sworn to give their ancestors, a land flowing with milk and honey. They came in and took possession of it, but they did not obey you or follow your law; they did not do what you commanded them to do. So you brought all this disaster on them...."

Then the word of the LORD came to Jeremiah: "I am the LORD, the God of all mankind. Is anything too hard for me? Therefore this is what the LORD says: I am about to give this city into the hands of the Babylonians and to Nebuchadnezzar king of Babylon, who will capture it. The Babylonians who are attacking this city will come in and set it on fire; they will burn it down, along with the houses where the people aroused my anger by burning incense on the roofs to Baal and by pouring out drink offerings to other gods.

"The people of Israel and Judah have done nothing but evil in my sight from their youth; indeed, the people of Israel have done nothing but arouse my anger with what their hands have made, declares the LORD."

JEREMIAH 32:17–23; 26–30

You show love to thousands
but bring the punishment for the parents' sin
into the laps of their children after them.
JEREMIAH 32:18-19

In books and sermons, Christians are often asked whether their faith is strong enough to withstand bad times. I wonder, though, if a better question is this: "Is my faith strong enough to survive good times?"

I keep hearing about people who drift away from the Lord not when life is bad but when it's good. That's when God seems unnecessary.

Too often we interpret His blessing as an indication of our goodness, not His. We assume we deserve everything pleasant that happens, and we fail to appreciate what He is telling us about himself through the good gifts He lets us enjoy.

In *The Problem of Pain*, C. S. Lewis wrote, "God whispers to us in our pleasures ... but shouts in our pains." If we refuse to listen when He whispers to us, He may use shouts to get our attention. That happened to the Israelites. Although God had given them "a land flowing with milk and honey," they turned from Him, so He "brought all this disaster on them" (Jeremiah 32:22–23).

The goodness of God is a reason to obey Him, not an opportunity to disobey. When we realize that, our relationship with the Lord will be strengthened, not weakened, by His wonderful bounty and blessing.

The goodness of God speaks volumes about His character.

Since, then, you have been raised with Christ, set your hearts on things above, where Christ is, seated at the right hand of God. Set your minds on things above, not on earthly things. For you died, and your life is now hidden with Christ in God. When Christ, who is your life, appears, then you also will appear with him in glory.

Put to death, therefore, whatever belongs to your earthly nature: sexual immorality, impurity, lust, evil desires and greed, which is idolatry. Because of these, the wrath of God is coming. You used to walk in these ways, in the life you once lived. But now you must also rid yourselves of all such things as these: anger, rage, malice, slander, and filthy language from your lips. Do not lie to each other, since you have taken off your old self with its practices and have put on the new self, which is being renewed in knowledge in the image of its Creator. Here there is no Gentile or Jew, circumcised or uncircumcised, barbarian, Scythian, slave or free, but Christ is all, and is in all.

Therefore, as God's chosen people, holy and dearly loved, clothe yourselves with compassion, kindness, humility, gentleness and patience. Bear with each other and forgive one another if any of you has a grievance against someone. Forgive as the Lord forgave you. And over all these virtues put on love, which binds them all together in perfect unity.

COLOSSIANS 3:1–14

Love the Lord your God with all your heart
and with all your soul and with all your mind
and with all your strength.
MARK 12:30

To detect health problems before they become serious, doctors recommend a routine physical exam. We can do the same for our spiritual health by asking a few questions rooted in the great commandment (Mark 12:30) Jesus referred to.

Do I love God with all my heart because He first loved me? Which is stronger, my desire for earthly gain or the treasures that are mine in Christ? (Colossians 3:1). He desires that His peace rule our hearts.

Do I love God with all my soul? Do I listen to God telling me who I am? Am I moving away from self-centered desires? (v. 5). Am I becoming more compassionate, kind, humble, gentle, and patient? (v. 12).

Do I love God with all my mind? Do I focus on my relationship with His Son or do I let my mind wander wherever it wants to go? (v. 2). Do my thoughts lead to problems or solutions? To unity or division? Forgiveness or revenge? (v. 13).

Do I love God with all my strength? Am I willing to be seen as weak so that God can show His strength on my behalf? (v. 17). Am I relying on His grace to be strong in His Spirit?

As we let "the message of Christ dwell among [us] richly ... with all wisdom" (v. 16), He will equip us to build each other up as we become spiritually fit and useful to Him.

**To be spiritually fit,
feed on God's Word and exercise your faith.**

*Now King David was told, "The L*ORD *has blessed the household of Obed-Edom and everything he has, because of the ark of God." So David went to bring up the ark of God from the house of Obed-Edom to the City of David with rejoicing. When those who were carrying the ark of the L*ORD *had taken six steps, he sacrificed a bull and a fattened calf. Wearing a linen ephod, David was dancing before the L*ORD *with all his might, while he and all Israel were bringing up the ark of the L*ORD *with shouts and the sound of trumpets.*

*As the ark of the L*ORD *was entering the City of David, Michal daughter of Saul watched from a window. And when she saw King David leaping and dancing before the L*ORD*, she despised him in her heart.*

*They brought the ark of the L*ORD *and set it in its place inside the tent that David had pitched for it, and David sacrificed burnt offerings and fellowship offerings before the L*ORD*. After he had finished sacrificing the burnt offerings and fellowship offerings, he blessed the people in the name of the L*ORD *Almighty. Then he gave a loaf of bread, a cake of dates and a cake of raisins to each person in the whole crowd of Israelites, both men and women. And all the people went to their homes.*

When David returned home to bless his household, Michal daughter of Saul came out to meet him and said, "How the king of Israel has distinguished himself today, going around half-naked in full view of the slave girls of his servants as any vulgar fellow would!"

*David said to Michal, "It was before the L*ORD*, who chose me rather than your father or anyone from his house when he appointed me ruler over the L*ORD*'s people Israel—I will celebrate before the L*ORD*. I will become even more undignified than this, and I will be humiliated in my own eyes. But by these slave girls you spoke of, I will be held in honor."*

And Michal daughter of Saul had no children to the day of her death.

2 SAMUEL 6:12–23

*Clap your hands, all you nations; shout to God
with cries of joy. For the LORD Most High is awesome,
the great King over all the earth.*
PSALM 47:1-2

On the left side of the aisle three people sat stiffly in the pew; on the right side sat a man in a wheelchair. When the congregation stood to sing, the man on the right had someone help him stand. The three on the left had their arms folded; the man on the right strained to lift his weak arms toward heaven. As the music swelled to a crescendo, the man on the right closed his eyes and struggled to make his mouth form the words of the familiar song; the three on the left stared straight ahead, their lips sealed.

Obviously I do not know the hearts of anyone in this story, but when I heard it, I knew I had to examine my own. The story reminded me that I often do more pouting than praising in church. Instead of concentrating on the God I worship, I often criticize the way others are worshiping.

When King David worshiped the Lord exuberantly, his wife called him shameless. He said, "I will become more undignified than this, and I will be humiliated in my own eyes" (2 Samuel 6:22). He knew that being God-conscious couldn't coexist with being self-conscious.

Taking worship seriously means taking ourselves less seriously. Worship is not about holding on to our dignity; it's about letting loose our praise.

We can never praise God too much!

Put to death, therefore, whatever belongs to your earthly nature: sexual immorality, impurity, lust, evil desires and greed, which is idolatry. Because of these, the wrath of God is coming. You used to walk in these ways, in the life you once lived. But now you must also rid yourselves of all such things as these: anger, rage, malice, slander, and filthy language from your lips. Do not lie to each other, since you have taken off your old self with its practices.

COLOSSIANS 3:5–9

"In your anger do not sin":
Do not let the sun go down
while you are still angry.
EPHESIANS 4:26

"How did everything get so dirty so fast?" I grumbled as I dusted the glass tabletop. "I had the whole house clean a month ago."

"Cleaning is a way of life, not an event," my husband responded.

I know he's right, but I hate to admit it. I want to clean the house once and have it stay that way. But dirt doesn't surrender that easily. Speck by speck, the dust returns. Piece by piece, the clutter piles up.

Sin is like the dust and clutter in my house. I want to eliminate all of it with one prayer of confession and repentance. But sin doesn't surrender that easily. Thought by thought, bad attitudes return. Choice by choice, unpleasant consequences pile up.

The apostle Paul told the believers in Colosse to get rid of "anger, rage, malice, slander, and filthy language" (Colossians 3:8). And he told the church at Ephesus, " 'In your anger do not sin': Do not let the sun go down while you are still angry" (Ephesians 4:26).

Christ's death and resurrection eliminated the need for daily sacrifice. But confession and repentance are still essential to the Christian's daily life. Getting rid of such things as anger, rage, and malice is a way of life, not a one-time event.

The best eraser in the world
is an honest confession to God.

Love must be sincere. Hate what is evil; cling to what is good. Be devoted to one another in love. Honor one another above yourselves. Never be lacking in zeal, but keep your spiritual fervor, serving the Lord. Be joyful in hope, patient in affliction, faithful in prayer. Share with the Lord's people who are in need. Practice hospitality.

Bless those who persecute you; bless and do not curse. Rejoice with those who rejoice; mourn with those who mourn. Live in harmony with one another. Do not be proud, but be willing to associate with people of low position. Do not be conceited.

Do not repay anyone evil for evil. Be careful to do what is right in the eyes of everyone.

If it is possible, as far as it depends on you, live at peace with everyone. Do not take revenge, my dear friends, but leave room for God's wrath, for it is written: "It is mine to avenge; I will repay," says the Lord. On the contrary:

> *"If your enemy is hungry, feed him;*
> *if he is thirsty, give him something to drink.*
> *In doing this, you will heap burning coals on his head."*

Do not be overcome by evil, but overcome evil with good.

ROMANS 12:9–21

Never be lacking in zeal,
but keep your spiritual fervor,
serving the Lord.
ROMANS 12:11

Modern furnaces have taken the work out of keeping warm in cold climates. We simply set the timer on the thermostat, and the house is warm when we get up in the morning. But in former days, fire was carefully tended and fuel supplies were closely monitored. Running out could be deadly.

The same is true spiritually. If we think our "spiritual fire" can be ignited as easily as a modern furnace, we risk losing our fervor for the Lord.

In ancient Israel, the priests were instructed not to let the fire on the altar go out (Leviticus 6:9, 12–13). This required a lot of work, not the least of which was collecting firewood in a land not known for its dense forests.

Some scholars see the fire on the altar as a symbol for the flame of our devotion for the Lord. Spiritual passion is not something to be treated lightly or taken for granted. It will grow cold if we fail to keep it supplied with fuel.

The apostle Paul addressed the subject of spiritual fervor in his letter to the Romans (12:1–2, 11). To keep the fire of our devotion burning strong, we must continue the hard work of stocking our fuel supply with hope, patience, steadfast prayer, generosity, hospitality, and humility (vv. 11–16).

Our love for Jesus
is the key to spiritual passion.

Peter, an apostle of Jesus Christ,

To God's elect, exiles scattered throughout the provinces of Pontus, Galatia, Cappadocia, Asia and Bithynia, who have been chosen according to the foreknowledge of God the Father, through the sanctifying work of the Spirit, to be obedient to Jesus Christ and sprinkled with his blood:
Grace and peace be yours in abundance.

Praise be to the God and Father of our Lord Jesus Christ! In his great mercy he has given us new birth into a living hope through the resurrection of Jesus Christ from the dead, and into an inheritance that can never perish, spoil or fade. This inheritance is kept in heaven for you, who through faith are shielded by God's power until the coming of the salvation that is ready to be revealed in the last time. In all this you greatly rejoice, though now for a little while you may have had to suffer grief in all kinds of trials. These have come so that the proven genuineness of your faith—of greater worth than gold, which perishes even though refined by fire—may result in praise, glory and honor when Jesus Christ is revealed. Though you have not seen him, you love him; and even though you do not see him now, you believe in him and are filled with an inexpressible and glorious joy, for you are receiving the end result of your faith, the salvation of your souls.

1 PETER 1:1–9

In their hearts humans plan their course,
but the LORD establishes their steps.
PROVERBS 16:9

My friend Linda grew up planning to become a medical missionary. She loves the Lord and wanted to serve Him as a doctor by taking the gospel to sick people in parts of the world where medical care is hard to find. But God had other plans. Linda has indeed become a medical missionary, but not the way she expected.

At age fourteen, Linda developed a chronic health problem that required her to be hospitalized for major surgery several times a year. She survived bacterial meningitis that left her in a coma for two weeks and blind for six months. She once celebrated two birthdays in a row in the hospital—without going home in between. She has had several experiences when she was not expected to live. But yet Linda is the most vibrant, grateful, and cheerful person you will ever meet. She once told me that her mission field, as she hoped and planned, is the hospital. But instead of serving God as a doctor, she serves Him as a patient. No matter how sick she is, the light of the Lord radiates from her.

Linda exemplifies the teaching of the apostle Peter. Despite her trials, she rejoices, and the genuineness of her faith brings "praise, honor, and glory" to Jesus Christ (1 Peter 1:6–7).

Write your plans in pencil
and remember that God has the eraser.

Be very careful, then, how you live—not as unwise but as wise, making the most of every opportunity, because the days are evil. Therefore do not be foolish, but understand what the Lord's will is. Do not get drunk on wine, which leads to debauchery. Instead, be filled with the Spirit, speaking to one another with psalms, hymns, and songs from the Spirit. Sing and make music from your heart to the Lord, always giving thanks to God the Father for everything, in the name of our Lord Jesus Christ.

Submit to one another out of reverence for Christ.

EPHESIANS 5:15–21

Always giving thanks to God the Father
for everything, in the name of our Lord Jesus Christ.
EPHESIANS 5:20

Interruptions are nothing new. Rarely does a day go by as planned.

Life is filled with inconveniences. Our plans are constantly thwarted by forces beyond our control. The list is long and ever changing: Sickness. Conflict. Traffic jams. Forgetfulness. Appliance malfunctions. Rudeness. Laziness. Impatience. Incompetence.

What we cannot see, however, is the other side of inconvenience. We think it has no purpose other than to discourage us, make life more difficult, and thwart our plans. However, inconvenience could be God's way of protecting us from some unseen danger, or it could be an opportunity to demonstrate God's grace and forgiveness. It might be the start of something even better than we had planned. Or it could be a test to see how we respond to adversity. Whatever it is, even though we may not know God's reason, we can be assured of His motive—to make us more like Jesus and to further His kingdom on earth.

To say that God's followers throughout history have been "inconvenienced" would be an understatement. But God had a purpose. Knowing this, we can thank Him, being confident that He is giving us an opportunity to redeem the time (Ephesians 5:16, 20).

What happens to us is not nearly as important as what God does in us and through us.

After this I looked, and there before me was a door standing open in heaven. And the voice I had first heard speaking to me like a trumpet said, "Come up here, and I will show you what must take place after this." At once I was in the Spirit, and there before me was a throne in heaven with someone sitting on it. And the one who sat there had the appearance of jasper and ruby. A rainbow that shone like an emerald encircled the throne. Surrounding the throne were twenty-four other thrones, and seated on them were twenty-four elders. They were dressed in white and had crowns of gold on their heads. From the throne came flashes of lightning, rumblings and peals of thunder. In front of the throne, seven lamps were blazing. These are the seven spirits of God. Also in front of the throne there was what looked like a sea of glass, clear as crystal.

In the center, around the throne, were four living creatures, and they were covered with eyes, in front and in back. The first living creature was like a lion, the second was like an ox, the third had a face like a man, the fourth was like a flying eagle. Each of the four living creatures had six wings and was covered with eyes all around, even under its wings. Day and night they never stop saying:

> *" 'Holy, holy, holy is the Lord God Almighty,'*
> *who was, and is, and is to come."*

Whenever the living creatures give glory, honor and thanks to him who sits on the throne and who lives for ever and ever, the twenty-four elders fall down before him who sits on the throne and worship him who lives for ever and ever. They lay their crowns before the throne and say:

> *"You are worthy, our Lord and God,*
> *to receive glory and honor and power,*
> *for you created all things,*
> *and by your will they were created*
> *and have their being."*

REVELATION 4

Each of the four living creatures had
six wings and was covered with eyes all around,
even under its wings.
REVELATION 4:8

"Time flies when you're having fun." This cliché has no basis in fact, but experience makes it seem true.

When life is pleasant, time passes all too quickly. Give me a task that I enjoy, or a person whose company I love, and time seems irrelevant.

My experience of this "reality" has given me a new understanding of the scene described in Revelation 4. In the past, when I considered the four living creatures seated around God's throne who keep repeating the same few words, I thought, *What a boring existence!*

I don't think that anymore. I think about the scenes they have witnessed with their many eyes (v. 8). I consider the view they have from their position around God's throne (v. 6). I think of how amazed they are at God's wise and loving involvement with wayward earthlings. Then I think, *What better response could there be? What else is there to say but, "Holy, holy, holy"?*

Is it boring to say the same words over and over? Not when you're in the presence of the one you love. Not when you're doing exactly what you were designed to do.

Like the four creatures, we were designed to glorify God. Our lives will never be boring if we're focusing our attention on Him and fulfilling that purpose.

**A heart in tune with God
can't help but sing His praise.**

PART 3

Hope for All Seasons

Then the LORD said to Moses, "Now you will see what I will do to Pharaoh: Because of my mighty hand he will let them go; because of my mighty hand he will drive them out of his country."

God also said to Moses, "I am the LORD. I appeared to Abraham, to Isaac and to Jacob as God Almighty, but by my name the LORD I did not make myself fully known to them. I also established my covenant with them to give them the land of Canaan, where they resided as foreigners. Moreover, I have heard the groaning of the Israelites, whom the Egyptians are enslaving, and I have remembered my covenant.

"Therefore, say to the Israelites: 'I am the LORD, and I will bring you out from under the yoke of the Egyptians. I will free you from being slaves to them, and I will redeem you with an outstretched arm and with mighty acts of judgment. I will take you as my own people, and I will be your God. Then you will know that I am the LORD your God, who brought you out from under the yoke of the Egyptians. And I will bring you to the land I swore with uplifted hand to give to Abraham, to Isaac and to Jacob. I will give it to you as a possession. I am the LORD.'"

Moses reported this to the Israelites, but they did not listen to him because of their discouragement and harsh labor.

EXODUS 6:1–9

But Jesus immediately said to them:
"Take courage! It is I. Don't be afraid."
MATTHEW 14:27

Scientists in the UK have calculated that the most depressing day of the year comes in the third week of January. Winter days are dark and cold, holiday excitement has worn off just as Christmas debts are coming due, and New Year's resolutions have all been broken. The celebrations, gift-giving, and good intentions that once made us feel happy now press us down and leave us feeling hopeless.

Long ago in Egypt, the Hebrew people had high hopes that Moses was going to rescue them from slavery. But their hopes were dashed when the good intentions of Moses led to worse conditions for them. Instead of gaining freedom, the people were pressed even harder by slave drivers who demanded that they produce more bricks with fewer resources.

Moses cried out to the Lord, "Since I went to Pharaoh to speak in your name, he has brought trouble on this people, and you have not rescued your people at all" (Exodus 5:23). As Moses and the Hebrew people were about to learn, God's rescue plans sometimes don't kick in until all hope seems to be gone.

If the circumstances of your life seem to be going from bad to worse, sending you into depression and despair, remember that God always hears and answers our cries—but it's in His time, not ours.

**When you feel hopeless,
look to the God of hope.**

In the beginning was the Word, and the Word was with God, and the Word was God. He was with God in the beginning. Through him all things were made; without him nothing was made that has been made. In him was life, and that life was the light of all mankind. The light shines in the darkness, and the darkness has not overcome it.

There was a man sent from God whose name was John. He came as a witness to testify concerning that light, so that through him all might believe. He himself was not the light; he came only as a witness to the light.

The true light that gives light to everyone was coming into the world.

JOHN 1:1–9

He came as a witness to testify concerning that light,
so that through him all might believe.
JOHN 1:7

The cozy little village of Rjukan, Norway, is a delightful place to live—except during the dark days of winter. Located in a valley at the foot of the towering Gaustatoppen Mountain, the town receives no direct sunlight for nearly half of the year. Residents had long considered the idea of placing mirrors at the top of the mountain to reflect the sun. But the concept was not feasible until recent years. In 2005, a local artist began "The Mirror Project" to bring together people who could turn the idea into reality. Eight years later, in October 2013, the mirrors went into action. Residents crowded into the town square to soak up the reflected sunlight.

In a spiritual sense, much of the world is like the village of Rjukan—mountains of troubles keep the light of Jesus from getting through. But God strategically places His children to act as reflectors. One such person was John the Baptist, who came "to bear witness of the Light"—Jesus—who gives light "to those who sit in darkness and the shadow of death" (John 1:7 NKJV; Luke 1:79 NKJV).

Just as sunlight is essential for emotional and physical health, so exposure to the light of Jesus is essential for spiritual health. Thankfully, every believer is in a position to reflect His light into the world's dark places.

**A world in darkness needs
the light of Jesus.**

When I went up on the mountain to receive the tablets of stone, the tablets of the covenant that the LORD *had made with you, I stayed on the mountain forty days and forty nights; I ate no bread and drank no water. The* LORD *gave me two stone tablets inscribed by the finger of God. On them were all the commandments the* LORD *proclaimed to you on the mountain out of the fire, on the day of the assembly.*

At the end of the forty days and forty nights, the LORD *gave me the two stone tablets, the tablets of the covenant. Then the* LORD *told me, "Go down from here at once, because your people whom you brought out of Egypt have become corrupt. They have turned away quickly from what I commanded them and have made an idol for themselves."*

And the LORD *said to me, "I have seen this people, and they are a stiff-necked people indeed! Let me alone, so that I may destroy them and blot out their name from under heaven. And I will make you into a nation stronger and more numerous than they."*

So I turned and went down from the mountain while it was ablaze with fire. And the two tablets of the covenant were in my hands. When I looked, I saw that you had sinned against the LORD *your God; you had made for yourselves an idol cast in the shape of a calf. You had turned aside quickly from the way that the* LORD *had commanded you.*

DEUTERONOMY 9:9–16

*Then the LORD told me,
"Go down from here at once, because your people
whom you brought out of Egypt have become corrupt."*
DEUTERONOMY 9:12

Thanks to the Internet, I can watch ice building up on Lake Michigan from my warm office thirty miles away. The changing angle of the sun's rays in winter chills the earth. Frigid temperatures turn surging water into rock-hard ice in a surprisingly short time. Witnessing this rapid transition reminds me of how quickly our hearts can turn cool toward God.

That happened to the ancient Israelites. After God miraculously rescued them from slavery, they became impatient when Moses climbed Mount Sinai to meet God and didn't return according to their timetable. So they got together and created their own god (Exodus 32:1). The Lord told Moses to hurry back down the mountain because the people had so quickly turned away (Deuteronomy 9:12).

When situations don't unfold according to our timetable, we might assume that God has lost interest in us. When we no longer feel close to Him, our hearts may grow cold. But God is always with us. As the psalmist wrote, "Where can I go from your Spirit? Where can I flee from your presence?" (Psalm 139:7).

Even when God seems distant, He's not. His presence fills heaven and earth (vv. 8–10). There's never a reason to let our hearts freeze over.

**The question is not where is God,
but where isn't He?**

There is a time for everything,
and a season for every activity under the heavens:

a time to be born and a time to die,
a time to plant and a time to uproot,
a time to kill and a time to heal,
a time to tear down and a time to build,
a time to weep and a time to laugh,
a time to mourn and a time to dance,
a time to scatter stones and a time to gather them,
a time to embrace and a time to refrain from embracing,
a time to search and a time to give up,
a time to keep and a time to throw away,
a time to tear and a time to mend,
a time to be silent and a time to speak,
a time to love and a time to hate,
a time for war and a time for peace.

What do workers gain from their toil? I have seen the burden
God has laid on the human race. He has made everything beau-
tiful in its time. He has also set eternity in the human heart; yet
no one can fathom what God has done from beginning to end. I
know that there is nothing better for people than to be happy and
to do good while they live. That each of them may eat and drink,
and find satisfaction in all their toil—this is the gift of God.
ECCLESIASTES 3:1–13

*I know that there is nothing better for people
than to be happy and to do good while they live.*
ECCLESIASTES 3:12

It's been a long, cold winter, and I am eager for warm weather. I'm tired of seeing bare trees and lifeless brown leaves covering the ground. I long to see wildflowers poke through the dead leaves and to watch the woods turn green once more.

Yet even as I anticipate my favorite season, I hear my mother's voice saying, "Don't wish your life away."

If you're like me, you sometimes hear yourself saying, "When such and such happens, then I will ..." or, "If only so and so would do this, then I would do that ..." or, "I would be happy if ..." or, "I will be satisfied when ..."

In longing for some future good, we forget that every day—regardless of the weather or our circumstances—is a gift from God to be used for His glory.

According to author Ron Ash, "We are where we need to be and learning what we need to learn. Stay the course because the things we experience today will lead us to where He needs us to be tomorrow."

In every season, there is a reason to rejoice and an opportunity to do good (Ecclesiastes 3:12). The challenge for each of us every day is to find something to rejoice about and some good to do—and then to do both.

**Every season brings
a reason to rejoice.**

So then he told them plainly, "Lazarus is dead, and for your sake I am glad I was not there, so that you may believe. But let us go to him."

Then Thomas (also known as Didymus) said to the rest of the disciples, "Let us also go, that we may die with him."

On his arrival, Jesus found that Lazarus had already been in the tomb for four days. Now Bethany was less than two miles from Jerusalem, and many Jews had come to Martha and Mary to comfort them in the loss of their brother. When Martha heard that Jesus was coming, she went out to meet him, but Mary stayed at home.

"Lord," Martha said to Jesus, "if you had been here, my brother would not have died. But I know that even now God will give you whatever you ask."

Jesus said to her, "Your brother will rise again."

Martha answered, "I know he will rise again in the resurrection at the last day."

Jesus said to her, "I am the resurrection and the life. The one who believes in me will live, even though they die; and whoever lives by believing in me will never die. Do you believe this?"

"Yes, Lord," she replied, "I believe that you are the Messiah, the Son of God, who is to come into the world."

JOHN 11:14–27

Jesus said to her, "I am the resurrection and the life.
The one who believes in me will live, even though they die;
and whoever lives by believing in me will never die."
JOHN 11:25

Through cold, snowy winters, the hope of spring sustains those of us who live in Michigan. May is the month when that hope is rewarded. The transformation is remarkable. Limbs that look lifeless on May 1 turn into branches that wave green leafy greetings by month's end. Although the change each day is imperceptible, by the end of the month the woods in my yard have changed from gray to green.

God has built into creation a cycle of rest and renewal. What looks like death to us is rest to God. And just as rest is preparation for renewal, death is preparation for resurrection.

I love watching the woods awaken every spring, for it reminds me that death is a temporary condition and that its purpose is to prepare for new life, a new beginning— for something even better. "Unless a kernel of wheat falls to the ground and dies, it remains only a single seed. But if it dies, it produces many seeds" (John 12:24).

While pollen is a springtime nuisance when it coats my furniture and makes people sneeze, it reminds me that God is in the business of keeping things alive. And after the pain of death, He promises a glorious resurrection for those who believe in His Son.

Every new leaf of springtime
is a reminder of our promised resurrection.

After Job had prayed for his friends, the LORD *restored his fortunes and gave him twice as much as he had before. All his brothers and sisters and everyone who had known him before came and ate with him in his house. They comforted and consoled him over all the trouble the* LORD *had brought on him, and each one gave him a piece of silver and a gold ring.*

The LORD *blessed the latter part of Job's life more than the former part. He had fourteen thousand sheep, six thousand camels, a thousand yoke of oxen and a thousand donkeys. And he also had seven sons and three daughters. The first daughter he named Jemimah, the second Keziah and the third Keren-Happuch. Nowhere in all the land were there found women as beautiful as Job's daughters, and their father granted them an inheritance along with their brothers.*

After this, Job lived a hundred and forty years; he saw his children and their children to the fourth generation. And so Job died, an old man and full of years.

JOB 42:10–17

The Lord blessed the latter part of Job's life
more than the former part.
JOB 42:12

Spring is the time of year when God reminds us that things are not always as they seem. Over the course of a few short weeks, what appears hopelessly dead comes to life. Bleak woodlands are transformed into colorful landscapes. Trees whose naked arms reached to heaven all winter, as if pleading to be clothed, are suddenly adorned with lacy green gowns. Flowers that faded and fell to the ground in surrender to the cold rise slowly from the earth in defiance of death.

In Scripture, we read about some apparently hopeless situations. One example is that of a wealthy man named Job whom God described as having integrity (Job 2:3). Disaster struck and Job lost everything important to him. In misery, he said, "My days ... come to an end without hope" (7:6). What appeared to Job and his friends as evidence that God had turned against him was just the opposite. God was so confident of Job's integrity that He trusted him in this battle with Satan. Later, Job's hope and life were renewed.

The faithful arrival of spring every year comforts me when I'm in a situation that seems hopeless. With God, there is no such thing. No matter how bleak the landscape of life may look, God can transform it into a glorious garden of color and fragrance.

**With God,
there is hope even in the most
hopeless situation.**

King Solomon was greater in riches and wisdom than all the other kings of the earth.

The whole world sought audience with Solomon to hear the wisdom God had put in his heart. Year after year, everyone who came brought a gift—articles of silver and gold, robes, weapons and spices, and horses and mules.

Solomon accumulated chariots and horses; he had fourteen hundred chariots and twelve thousand horses, which he kept in the chariot cities and also with him in Jerusalem. The king made silver as common in Jerusalem as stones, and cedar as plentiful as sycamore-fig trees in the foothills. Solomon's horses were imported from Egypt and from Kue—the royal merchants purchased them from Kue at the current price. They imported a chariot from Egypt for six hundred shekels of silver, and a horse for a hundred and fifty. They also exported them to all the kings of the Hittites and of the Arameans.

1 KINGS 10:23–29

King Solomon, however, loved many foreign women besides Pharaoh's daughter—Moabites, Ammonites, Edomites, Sidonians and Hittites. They were from nations about which the LORD *had told the Israelites, "You must not intermarry with them, because they will surely turn your hearts after their gods." Nevertheless, Solomon held fast to them in love. He had seven hundred wives of royal birth and three hundred concubines, and his wives led him astray. As Solomon grew old, his wives turned his heart after other gods, and his heart was not fully devoted to the* LORD *his God, as the heart of David his father had been.*

1 KINGS 11:1–4

*And the priests could not perform their service
because of the cloud,
for the glory of the LORD filled his temple.*
1 KINGS 8:11

Every year when May rolls around in Michigan, I want to stop the clock. I rejoice when death is defeated by fragile sprouts that refuse to be confined by hardened clay and brittle branches. Over a few weeks, the naked landscape transforms into fully clothed trees adorned by bright, fragrant flowers. I can't get enough of the sights, sounds, and scents of springtime. I want time to stop moving.

Also in May, I come to 1 Kings in my Bible reading schedule. When I get to chapter 10, I have the same feeling: I want the story to stop. The nation of Israel has bloomed. Solomon has become king and has built a magnificent dwelling place for God, who moved in with a blaze of glory (8:11). Finally united under a righteous king, they are at peace. I love happy endings!

But the story doesn't end there. It continues: "But King Solomon loved many foreign women" (11:1), and "his wives turned his heart after other gods" (v. 4).

Just as the seasons of the year continue, so do the cycles of life—birth and death, success and failure, sin and confession. Although we have no power to stop the clock while we're enjoying good times, we can rest in God's promise that eventually all bad times will end (Revelation 21:4).

**In good times and bad,
God never changes.**

Observe therefore all the commands I am giving you today, so that you may have the strength to go in and take over the land that you are crossing the Jordan to possess, and so that you may live long in the land the LORD swore to your ancestors to give to them and their descendants, a land flowing with milk and honey. The land you are entering to take over is not like the land of Egypt, from which you have come, where you planted your seed and irrigated it by foot as in a vegetable garden. But the land you are crossing the Jordan to take possession of is a land of mountains and valleys that drinks rain from heaven. It is a land the LORD your God cares for; the eyes of the LORD your God are continually on it from the beginning of the year to its end.

So if you faithfully obey the commands I am giving you today—to love the LORD your God and to serve him with all your heart and with all your soul—then I will send rain on your land in its season, both autumn and spring rains, so that you may gather in your grain, new wine and olive oil. I will provide grass in the fields for your cattle, and you will eat and be satisfied.

DEUTERONOMY 11:8–15

The land you are crossing the Jordan to take possession
of is a land of mountains and valleys that drinks rain
from heaven. It is a land the LORD your God cares for.
DEUTERONOMY 11:11–12

Friends are starting to plan their summer vegetable gardens. Some get an early start by planting seeds indoors where they can control the conditions and provide the best environment for sprouting. After the danger of frost has passed, they will transplant the seedlings outdoors. Once the garden is planted, the work of weeding, feeding, watering, and guarding against rodents and insects begins. Producing food is a lot of work.

Moses reminded the Israelites of this before they entered the Promised Land. While living in Egypt, they had to do the hard work of irrigating crops by hand (Deuteronomy 11:10), but in the place where God was taking them He promised to ease their work by sending spring and autumn rains: "I will send rain on your land in its season, both autumn and spring rains" (v. 14). The only condition was that they "faithfully obey the commands" He gave them—"to love the LORD your God and to serve him with all your heart and with all your soul" (v. 13). The Lord was taking His people to a place where their obedience and His blessing would make them a light to those around them.

God wants the same for us and from us: He wants our love to be displayed in our obedience so that we might be His light to people around us. The love and obedience we have to offer, though, is far less than He deserves. But He is our provider, blessing us and enabling us to be a light that the world will notice.

**Loving God doesn't make life effortless,
but having His strength makes it easier.**

At Iconium Paul and Barnabas went as usual into the Jewish synagogue. There they spoke so effectively that a great number of Jews and Greeks believed. But the Jews who refused to believe stirred up the other Gentiles and poisoned their minds against the brothers. So Paul and Barnabas spent considerable time there, speaking boldly for the Lord, who confirmed the message of his grace by enabling them to perform signs and wonders. The people of the city were divided; some sided with the Jews, others with the apostles. There was a plot afoot among both Gentiles and Jews, together with their leaders, to mistreat them and stone them. But they found out about it and fled to the Lycaonian cities of Lystra and Derbe and to the surrounding country, where they continued to preach the gospel.

In Lystra there sat a man who was lame. He had been that way from birth and had never walked. He listened to Paul as he was speaking. Paul looked directly at him, saw that he had faith to be healed and called out, "Stand up on your feet!" At that, the man jumped up and began to walk.

When the crowd saw what Paul had done, they shouted in the Lycaonian language, "The gods have come down to us in human form!" Barnabas they called Zeus, and Paul they called Hermes because he was the chief speaker. The priest of Zeus, whose temple was just outside the city, brought bulls and wreaths to the city gates because he and the crowd wanted to offer sacrifices to them.

But when the apostles Barnabas and Paul heard of this, they tore their clothes and rushed out into the crowd ...

Then some Jews came from Antioch and Iconium and won the crowd over. They stoned Paul and dragged him outside the city, thinking he was dead. But after the disciples had gathered around him, he got up and went back into the city. The next day he and Barnabas left for Derbe.

ACTS 14:1–15; 19–20

"We must go through many hardships
to enter the kingdom of God."
ACTS 14:22

The buttercups in our backyard were unusually bright and beautiful due to the generous amount of spring rain God sent our way. I wanted to take some pictures of them before they faded, but I had trouble getting close enough because they were growing in a very soggy wetland. One sunny afternoon, I pulled on a pair of boots and trudged through briers and brambles toward the buttercup bog. Before I got any pictures, I got muddy feet, multiple scratches, and numerous bug bites. But seeing the buttercups made my temporary discomfort worthwhile.

Much of life is about "getting through" the trials and troubles that are inevitable in our sinful world. One of these trials is persecution. The disciples certainly found this to be true. They knew the good things that Jesus has ready for those who follow Him, but they met harsh resistance when they tried to tell others (Acts 14:5).

Those of us who have chosen God's way and who know from experience that it's "a more excellent way" (1 Corinthians 12:31 NKJV) will persevere even when we have to go through danger and difficulty. By doing so, we show others a beautiful picture of God's peace, mercy, and forgiveness. The joy that awaits will make our temporary discomfort worthwhile.

Earth—the land of trials;
heaven—the land of joys.

It pleased Darius to appoint 120 satraps to rule throughout the kingdom, with three administrators over them, one of whom was Daniel. The satraps were made accountable to them so that the king might not suffer loss. Now Daniel so distinguished himself among the administrators and the satraps by his exceptional qualities that the king planned to set him over the whole kingdom. At this, the administrators and the satraps tried to find grounds for charges against Daniel in his conduct of government affairs, but they were unable to do so. They could find no corruption in him, because he was trustworthy and neither corrupt nor negligent. Finally these men said, "We will never find any basis for charges against this man Daniel unless it has something to do with the law of his God."

So these administrators and satraps went as a group to the king and said: "May King Darius live forever! The royal administrators, prefects, satraps, advisers and governors have all agreed that the king should issue an edict and enforce the decree that anyone who prays to any god or human being during the next thirty days, except to you, Your Majesty, shall be thrown into the lions' den. Now, Your Majesty, issue the decree and put it in writing so that it cannot be altered—in accordance with the law of the Medes and Persians, which cannot be repealed." So King Darius put the decree in writing.

Now when Daniel learned that the decree had been published, he went home to his upstairs room where the windows opened toward Jerusalem. Three times a day he got down on his knees and prayed, giving thanks to his God, just as he had done before.

DANIEL 6:1–10

Let the morning bring me word
of your unfailing love,
for I have put my trust in you.
PSALM 143:8

Summer is my favorite season. I love the leisurely days when I can set aside some of my routines without feeling guilty. Doing new things, seeing new places, and allowing myself the time to take "the scenic route" revive my spirit and renew my enthusiasm for life and work.

But summer can also be a dangerous time of breaking good habits. Certain routines are good. They increase our efficiency and ensure that important things get done. After all, we need to have fixed times and places for certain things or the world would be chaotic. Creation is designed to operate on schedule, and, as part of it, so are we. We need food and sleep at regular intervals.

We sometimes hear legitimate warnings about allowing routines to turn into ruts. But the Bible indicates that having set times for certain things is good. David indicated that morning was the right time for him to praise God and ask for His direction (Psalm 5:3; 143:8). And Daniel prayed three times a day—not even allowing the threat of death to change his routine (Daniel 6:10).

While enjoying carefree days, we must not become careless about spending time with God. Savoring spiritual sustenance is a routine for all seasons.

Those who wait on the Lord
shall renew their strength.
—ISAIAH 40:31

When you are harvesting in your field and you overlook a sheaf, do not go back to get it. Leave it for the foreigner, the fatherless and the widow, so that the LORD *your God may bless you in all the work of your hands. When you beat the olives from your trees, do not go over the branches a second time. Leave what remains for the foreigner, the fatherless and the widow. When you harvest the grapes in your vineyard, do not go over the vines again. Leave what remains for the foreigner, the fatherless and the widow. Remember that you were slaves in Egypt. That is why I command you to do this.*

DEUTERONOMY 24:19–22

Those who work their land will have abundant food,
but those who chase fantasies have no sense.
PROVERBS 12:11

Outside my office window, the squirrels are in a race against winter to bury their acorns in a safe, accessible place. Their commotion amuses me. An entire herd of deer can go through our backyard and not make a sound, but one squirrel sounds like an invasion.

The two creatures are different in another way as well. Deer do not prepare for winter. When the snow comes, they eat whatever they can find along the way (including ornamental shrubs in our yard). But squirrels would starve if they followed that example. They would be unable to find suitable food.

The deer and the squirrel represent ways God cares for us. He enables us to work and save for the future, and He meets our need when resources are scarce. As the wisdom literature teaches, God gives us seasons of plenty so we can prepare for seasons of need (Proverbs 12:11). And as Psalm 23 says, the Lord leads us through perilous places to pleasant pastures.

Another way God provides is by instructing people with plenty to share with those in need (Deuteronomy 24:19). So when it comes to provision, the message of the Bible is this: Work while we can, save what we can, share what we can, and trust God to meet our needs.

Our needs will never
exhaust God's supply.

But if it is preached that Christ has been raised from the dead, how can some of you say that there is no resurrection of the dead? If there is no resurrection of the dead, then not even Christ has been raised. And if Christ has not been raised, our preaching is useless and so is your faith. More than that, we are then found to be false witnesses about God, for we have testified about God that he raised Christ from the dead. But he did not raise him if in fact the dead are not raised. For if the dead are not raised, then Christ has not been raised either. And if Christ has not been raised, your faith is futile; you are still in your sins. Then those also who have fallen asleep in Christ are lost. If only for this life we have hope in Christ, we are of all people most to be pitied.

But Christ has indeed been raised from the dead, the firstfruits of those who have fallen asleep.

1 CORINTHIANS 15:12–20

Here is a trustworthy saying:
If we died with him,
we will also live with him.
2 TIMOTHY 2:11

Inside, music was playing. Outside, leaves were falling. Catching a gust of wind, one of the last leaves of autumn blew briefly upward as I heard the phrase, "He is risen!" By the end of the song, however, the leaf had reached the ground. Gravity had overcome the breeze.

Later, I overheard three middle-aged women discussing diets, exercise, face-lifts, and other age-defying efforts. Like the leaf, they were trying to keep gravity from pulling them toward the inevitable.

Their conversation reminds me of the good works people do to try to save themselves from spiritual death. But just as leaves cannot keep from falling and people cannot keep from aging, no one can work hard enough to avoid the consequences of sin, which is death (Romans 6:23).

At the crucifixion, mockers challenged Jesus to save himself. Instead, He put His life into the hands of God, and God gave back to Him not only His own life but ours as well. To receive salvation, we too must simply put our lives into the hands of God. If the Spirit of Him who raised Jesus from the dead lives in us, He will give life to us as well (Romans 8:11).

The forces of sin outside cannot defeat the life of Christ inside.

Salvation isn't turning over a new leaf;
it's receiving a new life.

When the time came for the purification rites required by the Law of Moses, Joseph and Mary took [Jesus] to Jerusalem to present him to the Lord (as it is written in the Law of the Lord, "Every firstborn male is to be consecrated to the Lord"), and to offer a sacrifice in keeping with what is said in the Law of the Lord: "a pair of doves or two young pigeons."

Now there was a man in Jerusalem called Simeon, who was righteous and devout. He was waiting for the consolation of Israel, and the Holy Spirit was on him. It had been revealed to him by the Holy Spirit that he would not die before he had seen the Lord's Messiah. Moved by the Spirit, he went into the temple courts. When the parents brought in the child Jesus to do for him what the custom of the Law required,

Simeon took him in his arms and praised God, saying:

> *"Sovereign Lord, as you have promised, you may now dismiss your servant in peace. For my eyes have seen your salvation, which you have prepared in the sight of all nations: a light for revelation to the Gentiles, and the glory of your people Israel."*

The child's father and mother marveled at what was said about him. Then Simeon blessed them and said to Mary, his mother: "This child is destined to cause the falling and rising of many in Israel, and to be a sign that will be spoken against, so that the thoughts of many hearts will be revealed. And a sword will pierce your own soul too."

There was also a prophet, Anna, the daughter of Penuel, of the tribe of Asher. She was very old; she had lived with her husband seven years after her marriage, and then was a widow until she was eighty-four. She never left the temple but worshiped night and day, fasting and praying. Coming up to them at that very moment, she gave thanks to God and spoke about the child to all who were looking forward to the redemption of Jerusalem.

LUKE 2:22–38

The LORD longs to be gracious to you;
therefore he will rise up to show you compassion.
ISAIAH 30:18

Autumn is hunting season in Michigan where my husband, Jay, and I live. For a few weeks every year, licensed hunters are allowed to go out into the woods and hunt for various species of wildlife. Some hunters build elaborate tree stands high above the ground where they sit quietly for hours waiting for a deer to wander within rifle range.

When I think of hunters who are so patient when it comes to waiting for deer, I think of how impatient we can be when we have to wait for God. We often equate "wait" with "waste." If we're waiting for something (or someone), we think we are doing nothing, which, in an accomplishment-crazed culture, seems like a waste of time.

But waiting serves many purposes. In particular, it proves our faith. Those whose faith is weak are often the first to give up waiting, while those with the strongest faith are willing to wait indefinitely.

When we read the Christmas story in Luke 2, we learn of two people who proved their faith by their willingness to wait. Simeon and Anna waited long, but their time wasn't wasted; it put them in a place where they could witness the coming of Messiah (vv. 22–38).

Not receiving an immediate answer to prayer is no reason to give up faith.

Waiting for God
is never a waste of time.

So Moses wrote down this law and gave it to the Levitical priests, who carried the ark of the covenant of the LORD, and to all the elders of Israel. Then Moses commanded them: "At the end of every seven years, in the year for canceling debts, during the Festival of Tabernacles, when all Israel comes to appear before the LORD your God at the place he will choose, you shall read this law before them in their hearing.

"Assemble the people—men, women and children, and the foreigners residing in your towns—so they can listen and learn to fear the LORD your God and follow carefully all the words of this law. Their children, who do not know this law, must hear it and learn to fear the LORD your God as long as you live in the land you are crossing the Jordan to possess."

DEUTERONOMY 31:9–13

The Word became flesh and made
his dwelling among us. We have seen his glory,
the glory of the one and only Son,
who came from the Father, full of grace and truth.
JOHN 1:14

When Christmas displays go up before Halloween displays come down, I long for the days when people didn't think about Christmas until after Thanksgiving. However, there may be a legitimate reason to celebrate Christmas in October.

No one knows the exact day when Jesus was born, but December 25 is unlikely. His birth may have been in autumn, when the weather was still warm enough for shepherds to be outdoors with their flocks. We know that Jesus was crucified on Passover, and that the Holy Spirit came on Pentecost. So some scholars have reasoned that Jesus's birth may have occurred on another Jewish holiday, the Feast of Tabernacles, or Sukkot.

Although we cannot know for sure, we do know that it would be in keeping with God's way of working to send His Son—the Word made flesh who "dwelt" ("tabernacled") among us (John 1:14)—on the Feast of Tabernacles. Sukkot was a time when observant Jews lived in temporary dwellings and listened to the Word of the Lord being read (Deuteronomy 31:10–13).

For Jews, Sukkot is "the time of our rejoicing." For all of us, our time of rejoicing is the birth of Christ, who brings the joy of salvation to all the world.

**The date of Christ's birth may be debatable,
but the fact of His life is indisputable.**

PART 4

Hope in Beauty and Nature

"*Blessed are you when people insult you, persecute you and falsely say all kinds of evil against you because of me. Rejoice and be glad, because great is your reward in heaven, for in the same way they persecuted the prophets who were before you.*

"*You are the salt of the earth. But if the salt loses its saltiness, how can it be made salty again? It is no longer good for anything, except to be thrown out and trampled underfoot.*

"*You are the light of the world. A town built on a hill cannot be hidden. Neither do people light a lamp and put it under a bowl. Instead they put it on its stand, and it gives light to everyone in the house. In the same way, let your light shine before others, that they may see your good deeds and glorify your Father in heaven.*"

MATTHEW 5:11–16

Let your light shine before others,
that they may see your good deeds
and glorify your Father in heaven.
MATTHEW 5:16

The Lake Michigan shoreline (a short drive from where I live) is dotted with lighthouses built to enable ship captains to navigate into safe harbors. The structures are varied in size, shape, and color, but each has unique charm and beauty. Pictures of the lighthouses are featured in books and calendars, and some people collect replicas and other lighthouse items.

But lighthouses were not built just to be admired; they were built to hold lights that guide sailors to safety. A lighthouse is most useful and appreciated when, in the darkness of night, only its light can be seen—not the structure itself.

When Jesus sent out His disciples, He called them "the light of the world" (Matthew 5:14). He also indicated that their task was not to draw attention to themselves, but to do good works that would cause people to recognize God's goodness and glorify Him.

Jesus said that just as a lamp's purpose is to give light, we also are to let our light shine (vv. 15–16). We're most effective when we shine brightly in the darkness, guiding people who need to find safe harbor in Christ.

For a light to be effective, it has to be shining in a dark place.

A little light makes a big difference
in the darkest night.

David summoned all the officials of Israel to assemble at Jerusalem: the officers over the tribes, the commanders of the divisions in the service of the king, the commanders of thousands and commanders of hundreds, and the officials in charge of all the property and livestock belonging to the king and his sons, together with the palace officials, the warriors and all the brave fighting men.

King David rose to his feet and said: "Listen to me, my fellow Israelites, my people. I had it in my heart to build a house as a place of rest for the ark of the covenant of the LORD, for the footstool of our God, and I made plans to build it. But God said to me, 'You are not to build a house for my Name, because you are a warrior and have shed blood.'

"Yet the LORD, the God of Israel, chose me from my whole family to be king over Israel forever. He chose Judah as leader, and from the tribe of Judah he chose my family, and from my father's sons he was pleased to make me king over all Israel. Of all my sons—and the LORD has given me many—he has chosen my son Solomon to sit on the throne of the kingdom of the LORD over Israel. He said to me: 'Solomon your son is the one who will build my house and my courts, for I have chosen him to be my son, and I will be his father. I will establish his kingdom forever if he is unswerving in carrying out my commands and laws, as is being done at this time....'

"And you, my son Solomon, acknowledge the God of your father, and serve him with wholehearted devotion and with a willing mind, for the LORD searches every heart and understands every desire and every thought. If you seek him, he will be found by you; but if you forsake him, he will reject you forever. Consider now, for the LORD has chosen you to build a house as the sanctuary. Be strong and do the work."

1 CHRONICLES 28:1–7; 9–10

Solomon, acknowledge the God of your father,
and serve him with wholehearted devotion
and with a willing mind,
for the LORD searches every heart and
understands every desire and every thought.
If you seek him, he will be found by you.
1 CHRONICLES 28:9

Tourists rarely take great photographs. They seldom make the effort to be at the right spot at the right time to get the right angle of light in the right weather conditions. To capture beautiful outdoor pictures, professional photographers are careful to view the scene from different angles, during different seasons, and at different times of day.

This makes me wonder if the reason some people don't have a clear picture of the beauty and glory of God is that they make snap judgments. They come to wrong conclusions about God based on a bad church experience or an encounter with someone who claims to be a Christian but isn't living like one. They misjudge what the Lord is like and turn away from Him, feeling disillusioned.

The pursuit of God involves more than casual observation. King David told his son Solomon, "If you seek him, he will be found by you" (1 Chronicles 28:9). The psalmist said, "Blessed are those who … seek him with all their heart!" (Psalm 119:2). And the author of Hebrews wrote that God rewards "those who earnestly seek Him" (11:6).

To see and know God in all His fullness and glory, we can't approach Him like tourists. We need to seek Him at all times, with all our heart.

To find God,
we must be willing to seek Him.

But now you must also rid yourselves of all such things as these: anger, rage, malice, slander, and filthy language from your lips. Do not lie to each other, since you have taken off your old self with its practices and have put on the new self, which is being renewed in knowledge in the image of its Creator. Here there is no Gentile or Jew, circumcised or uncircumcised, barbarian, Scythian, slave or free, but Christ is all, and is in all.

Therefore, as God's chosen people, holy and dearly loved, clothe yourselves with compassion, kindness, humility, gentleness and patience. Bear with each other and forgive one another if any of you has a grievance against someone. Forgive as the Lord forgave you. And over all these virtues put on love, which binds them all together in perfect unity.

Let the peace of Christ rule in your hearts, since as members of one body you were called to peace. And be thankful. Let the message of Christ dwell among you richly as you teach and admonish one another with all wisdom through psalms, hymns, and songs from the Spirit, singing to God with gratitude in your hearts. And whatever you do, whether in word or deed, do it all in the name of the Lord Jesus, giving thanks to God the Father through him.

COLOSSIANS 3:8–17

Put on the new self,
which is being renewed in knowledge
in the image of its Creator.
COLOSSIANS 3:10

Vincent van Gogh bought a mirror and used his own likeness in many of his paintings. Rembrandt also used himself as a model, completing nearly 100 self-portraits. These artists had a good example—that of God himself, who used His own likeness as the pattern for His crown jewel of creation (Genesis 1:27).

Henry Ward Beecher, the famous nineteenth-century clergyman, said, "Every artist dips his brush in his own soul, and paints his own nature into his pictures." In everything we create—works of art, music, literature, even our children—a bit of ourselves is revealed. The same is true of God; each of us reveals a bit of Him. The image may be tarnished, but it's always there and is never beyond repair.

Superficial changes won't fix what's wrong with us, however. Clothes, cosmetics, and surgical procedures can make us look like everyone else, not like the unique masterpiece God designed each of us to be. We need a whole new "self" (Colossians 3:10), one that is renewed in His image and dressed in the wardrobe of mercy, kindness, humility, meekness, and longsuffering (v. 12).

To improve your "self" image, put on the character of God and display His image in all its glory.

God's children should reflect
their Father's likeness.

When he was gone, Jesus said, "Now the Son of Man is glorified and God is glorified in him. If God is glorified in him] God will glorify the Son in himself, and will glorify him at once.

"My children, I will be with you only a little longer. You will look for me, and just as I told the Jews, so I tell you now: Where I am going, you cannot come.

"A new command I give you: Love one another. As I have loved you, so you must love one another. By this everyone will know that you are my disciples, if you love one another."

Simon Peter asked him, "Lord, where are you going?"

Jesus replied, "Where I am going, you cannot follow now, but you will follow later."

Peter asked, "Lord, why can't I follow you now? I will lay down my life for you."

Then Jesus answered, "Will you really lay down your life for me? Very truly I tell you, before the rooster crows, you will disown me three times!"

JOHN 13:31–38

By this everyone will know
that you are my disciples,
if you love one another.
JOHN 13:35

David Doubilet is a photojournalist whose pictures of a silent underwater world can turn even an ugly, bug-eyed sea creature into a lovely, luminescent work of art. Although he has received many honors for his work, he has also been criticized by environmentalists for not doing more "hard-edged" journalism. They want him to take pictures of dead fish, dirty beaches, and polluted oceans.

But Doubilet believes there's a better way to get people to care about the environment. Instead of showing the destruction that humans are causing, he shows the beauty God has created.

Some Christians seem to think the way to improve our spiritual environment is to point out all the evil in the world. But Jesus showed us a better way. Although He never glossed over sin (Matthew 15:18–20), He said to His followers before going to the cross, "By this everyone will know that you are my disciples, if you love one another" (John 13:35). We are more effective witnesses when we become portraits of the beauty God is creating in us than when we merely paint a bleak picture of human degradation.

"In the end," says Doubilet, "the best thing one can do is to amaze people." And what could be more amazing to the world than Christians who truly love one another?

Love is a magnet
that draws believers together
and unbelievers to Christ.

Then Moses said to the Israelites, "See, the LORD has chosen Bezalel son of Uri, the son of Hur, of the tribe of Judah, and he has filled him with the Spirit of God, with wisdom, with understanding, with knowledge and with all kinds of skills— to make artistic designs for work in gold, silver and bronze, to cut and set stones, to work in wood and to engage in all kinds of artistic crafts. And he has given both him and Oholiab son of Ahisamak, of the tribe of Dan, the ability to teach others. He has filled them with skill to do all kinds of work as engravers, designers, embroiderers in blue, purple and scarlet yarn and fine linen, and weavers—all of them skilled workers and designers."

EXODUS 35:30–35

[God] has filled [Bezalel] with the Spirit of God,
with wisdom, with understanding,
with knowledge and with all kinds of skills.
EXODUS 35:31-32

"Why plant flowers? You can't eat them," said my father-in-law after witnessing my spring ritual of filling pots with fragrant and colorful treasures from the garden store. Jay's dad is an engineer—a practical sort of person. He can make anything work, but making it beautiful is not a priority. He values function over form, usefulness over aesthetics.

God created us with different gifts. Engineers who work for the glory of God design machines that make life easier. The Lord also created artists, who make life more pleasant by creating beautiful things for the glory of God and the enjoyment of others.

When we think of art in worship, we usually think of music. But other art forms have long had a role in glorifying God. The calling of Bezalel demonstrates God's regard for fine art (Exodus 35:30–35). God commissioned him to beautify the first official place of worship: the tabernacle. God's purpose for the arts, according to Gene Edward Veith, an expert on Christianity and culture, is "to glorify God and to manifest beauty."

When artistic talent is enlivened by the Spirit of God, it becomes an act of worship that then can become a witness to point people to Christ. God has greatly enriched our lives with beauty. And we in turn express our gratitude by displaying His glory in our art.

**Do all things
for the glory of God.**

"When Israel was a child, I loved him,
    and out of Egypt I called my son.
But the more they were called,
    the more they went away from me.
They sacrificed to the Baals
    and they burned incense to images.
It was I who taught Ephraim to walk,
    taking them by the arms;
but they did not realize
    it was I who healed them.
I led them with cords of human kindness,
    with ties of love.
To them I was like one who lifts
    a little child to the cheek,
    and I bent down to feed them.

"Will they not return to Egypt
    and will not Assyria rule over them
    because they refuse to repent?
A sword will flash in their cities;
    it will devour their false prophets
    and put an end to their plans.
My people are determined to turn from me.
    Even though they call me God Most High,
    I will by no means exalt them."

HOSEA 11:1–7

When I fed them, they were satisfied;
when they were satisfied, they became proud.
HOSEA 13:6

Guests probably wonder why I keep a scraggly fern in my living room. I've gotten so used to its unsightliness that I seldom think to explain. The plant symbolizes a friendship that has become fragile, and I keep it in a prominent place as a reminder to pray for my friend, which I do whenever I water it. Its dried leaves make it obvious that I don't water it often enough, which also means that I don't pray often enough for my friend.

My fern is drying up because I don't water it until it wilts, and I carry that attitude along with me into my spiritual life. As long as my life is not in crisis, I figure that prayer can wait a while. But I'm wrong. When God's blessings make me think I don't need Him, I am more needy than ever.

The book of Hosea summarizes God's relationship with His chosen nation in words that parallel my own spiritual experience. God blesses, I grow; God satisfies, I take credit; God withholds His blessing, I realize my neediness; God reveals my sin, I repent; God forgives, I renew my devotion.

I've learned from my plant that I must pray even when I don't see the need. I need God just as much when I'm being blessed as when I am in crisis.

**There is never a day
when you don't need to pray.**

"Therefore I tell you, do not worry about your life, what you will eat or drink; or about your body, what you will wear. Is not life more than food, and the body more than clothes? Look at the birds of the air; they do not sow or reap or store away in barns, and yet your heavenly Father feeds them. Are you not much more valuable than they? Can any one of you by worrying add a single hour to your life?

"And why do you worry about clothes? See how the flowers of the field grow. They do not labor or spin. Yet I tell you that not even Solomon in all his splendor was dressed like one of these. If that is how God clothes the grass of the field, which is here today and tomorrow is thrown into the fire, will he not much more clothe you—you of little faith? So do not worry, saying, 'What shall we eat?' or 'What shall we drink?' or 'What shall we wear?' For the pagans run after all these things, and your heavenly Father knows that you need them. But seek first his kingdom and his righteousness, and all these things will be given to you as well. Therefore do not worry about tomorrow, for tomorrow will worry about itself. Each day has enough trouble of its own."

MATTHEW 6:25–34

Look at the birds of the air;
they do not sow or reap or store away in barns,
and yet your heavenly Father feeds them.
Are you not much more valuable than they?
MATTHEW 6:26

Twig by twig a cardinal constructed a bowl-shaped home in the bush outside my office window. Soon she laid an egg and kept it warm until it hatched. I named the little bird Michael. Although he was tiny, he had a huge appetite. His parents worked hard to keep him fed and safe. In a few months, Michael was ready to leave, and I was there to witness the amazing event.

When Michael left, so did mom and dad. The nest remained empty until the next spring. When mama cardinal returned, I was happy to see her, but I was also sad. We had sold our house and I was concerned that the new owners might chop down the bush. But my concern soon turned to amazement. As I dismantled my office, mama cardinal dismantled her nest. By the time we left, so had the cardinal family. Mama cardinal's God-given instincts had told her to move.

This brought to mind another nature lesson. Using birds and lilies as examples, Jesus urged people not to worry. Since God takes care of birds, surely He will take care of His people (Matthew 6:26–30).

When concern for our own well-being leads to anxious thoughts, we can look at the birds and be assured of our value to God and of His care for us.

**Hope can be ignited
by a spark of encouragement.**

"Have you entered the storehouses of the snow
or seen the storehouses of the hail,
which I reserve for times of trouble,
for days of war and battle?
What is the way to the place where the lightning is dispersed,
or the place where the east winds are scattered over the earth?
Who cuts a channel for the torrents of rain,
and a path for the thunderstorm,
to water a land where no one lives,
an uninhabited desert,
to satisfy a desolate wasteland
and make it sprout with grass?
Does the rain have a father?
Who fathers the drops of dew?
From whose womb comes the ice?
Who gives birth to the frost from the heavens
when the waters become hard as stone,
when the surface of the deep is frozen?"

JOB 38:22–30

From whose womb comes the ice?
Who gives birth to the frost from the heavens
when the waters become hard as stone,
when the surface of the deep is frozen?
JOB 38:29-30

Loud creaking and snapping broke the stillness of the icy morning. Freezing rain had silenced every man-made noise-maker. Power lines were down; homes and businesses had no electricity. Roads were impassable, keeping thousands from daily routines. Nature was calling attention to herself, and she got it. As the sun rose, her stunning beauty was indescribable, her destructive power undeniable.

Ice glistened like crystal against a brilliant blue sky. But the ice that made the branches sparkle in the sunlight also weighed them down, causing them to break under the burden.

The same can happen to those who have glittering lives. They call attention to themselves with stunning beauty, talent, or intelligence. People notice and admire them. But eventually the weight of pride causes people to crack and break. The reality is that God alone is worthy of all praise.

Job's friends called attention to themselves by speaking as if they were experts on suffering. When God had heard enough, He pointed out to Job that no one has knowledge, power, or importance apart from Him. Later, He sharply rebuked Job's friends, and said, "You have not spoken the truth about me" (Job 42:8).

**True worth is in exalting God,
not ourselves.**

The heavens declare the glory of God;
  the skies proclaim the work of his hands.
Day after day they pour forth speech;
  night after night they reveal knowledge.
They have no speech, they use no words;
  no sound is heard from them.
Yet their voice goes out into all the earth,
  their words to the ends of the world.
In the heavens God has pitched a tent for the sun.
  It is like a bridegroom coming out of his chamber,
  like a champion rejoicing to run his course.
It rises at one end of the heavens
  and makes its circuit to the other;
  nothing is deprived of its warmth.

PSALM 19:1–6

The heavens declare the glory of God;
the skies proclaim the work of his hands.
PSALM 19:1

I enjoy nature and giving praise to its Creator, but I sometimes wrongly feel guilty for admiring it too much. Then I remember that Jesus used nature as a teaching tool. To encourage people not to worry, He used simple wildflowers as an example. "Consider the lilies" (Luke 12:27 KJV), He said, and then reminded people that even though flowers do no work at all, God dresses them in splendor. His conclusion? If God clothes something temporary in such glory, He surely will do much more for us (Matthew 6:28–34).

Other portions of Scripture indicate that creation is one of the ways God uses to tell us about himself:

"The heavens declare the glory of God; the skies proclaim the work of his hands," wrote David. "Day after day they pour forth speech; night they reveal knowledge" (Psalm 19:1–2).

"The heavens proclaim his righteousness, for he is a God of justice," Asaph said (50:6).

And Paul wrote, "For since the creation of the world God's invisible qualities—his eternal power and divine nature— have been clearly seen, being understood from what has been made, so that people are without excuse" (Romans 1:20).

God so loves us and wants us to know Him that He put evidence of himself everywhere we look.

In God's pattern book of nature
we can trace many valuable lessons.

That same day Jesus went out of the house and sat by the lake. Such large crowds gathered around him that he got into a boat and sat in it, while all the people stood on the shore. Then he told them many things in parables, saying: "A farmer went out to sow his seed. As he was scattering the seed, some fell along the path, and the birds came and ate it up. Some fell on rocky places, where it did not have much soil. It sprang up quickly, because the soil was shallow. But when the sun came up, the plants were scorched, and they withered because they had no root. Other seed fell among thorns, which grew up and choked the plants. Still other seed fell on good soil, where it produced a crop—a hundred, sixty or thirty times what was sown. Whoever has ears, let them hear."

MATTHEW 13:1–9

But when the sun came up,
the plants were scorched,
and they withered because
they had no root.
MATTHEW 13:6

In the life of trees, one key to survival is having more roots than shoots. In his book *Oak: The Frame of Civilization*, author William Bryant Logan says, "If a tree puts on a lot of top growth and few roots, it is liable to be weak-wooded and short-lived.... If a tree puts down a great deal of roots and adds shoots more slowly, however, it is liable to be long-lived and more resistant to stress and strain."

People and organizations can be like trees. The rise to prominence is exhilarating, but anything that puts up shoots faster than it puts down roots is fragile and in danger of breaking, falling, or dying.

Jesus used a similar analogy in His parable of the sower. People who hear the Word and receive it joyfully are like seed sown on stony places; they spring up quickly but endure only a short time because they have no roots (Matthew 13:6, 20–21).

Roots aren't at all glamorous, but they are the source of our strength. If our roots go deep in the knowledge of God (Jeremiah 9:24) and our lives are hidden in Christ (Colossians 3:3), we'll be strong, resistant to blight, and more likely to survive the storms of adversity.

How deep are your roots?

The word of the LORD came to Jonah son of Amittai: "Go to the great city of Nineveh and preach against it, because its wickedness has come up before me."

But Jonah ran away from the LORD and headed for Tarshish. He went down to Joppa, where he found a ship bound for that port. After paying the fare, he went aboard and sailed for Tarshish to flee from the LORD.

Then the LORD sent a great wind on the sea, and such a violent storm arose that the ship threatened to break up. All the sailors were afraid and each cried out to his own god. And they threw the cargo into the sea to lighten the ship.

But Jonah had gone below deck, where he lay down and fell into a deep sleep. The captain went to him and said, "How can you sleep? Get up and call on your god! Maybe he will take notice of us so that we will not perish."

Then the sailors said to each other, "Come, let us cast lots to find out who is responsible for this calamity." They cast lots and the lot fell on Jonah. So they asked him, "Tell us, who is responsible for making all this trouble for us? What kind of work do you do? Where do you come from? What is your country? From what people are you?"

He answered, "I am a Hebrew and I worship the LORD, the God of heaven, who made the sea and the dry land."

This terrified them and they asked, "What have you done?" (They knew he was running away from the LORD, because he had already told them so.)

The sea was getting rougher and rougher. So they asked him, "What should we do to you to make the sea calm down for us?"

"Pick me up and throw me into the sea," he replied,... Then they took Jonah and threw him overboard, and the raging sea grew calm. At this the men greatly feared the LORD, and they offered a sacrifice to the LORD and made vows to him.

Now the LORD provided a huge fish to swallow Jonah, and Jonah was in the belly of the fish three days and three nights.

JONAH 1:1–12; 15–17

Get rid of all bitterness, rage and anger,
brawling and slander,
along with every form of malice.
EPHESIANS 4:31

God did some fall housecleaning this week. He sent a mighty wind through our neighborhood that made the trees tremble and shake loose their dead branches. When it finished, I had a mess to clean up.

In my own life, God sometimes works in a similar way. He will send or allow stormy circumstances that shake loose the "lifeless branches" I've been refusing to release. Sometimes it's something that once was good, like an area of ministry, but is no longer bearing fruit. More often it's something that's not good, like a bad habit I've slid into or a stubborn attitude that prevents new growth.

The Old Testament prophet Jonah discovered what can happen when one refuses to get rid of a stubborn attitude. His hatred for the Ninevites was stronger than his love for God, so God sent a great storm that landed Jonah in a giant fish (Jonah 1:4, 17). God preserved the reluctant prophet in that unlikely place and gave him a second chance to obey (2:10; 3:1–3).

The lifeless limbs in my yard caused me to think of attitudes that God expects me to dispose of. Paul's letter to the Ephesians lists some of them: bitterness, anger, and evil speech (4:31). When God shakes things up, we need to get rid of what He shakes loose.

Christ's cleansing power can remove
the most stubborn stain of sin.

Then the L*ORD* *was jealous for his land*
and took pity on his people.

The L*ORD* *replied to them:*

"I am sending you grain, new wine and olive oil,
enough to satisfy you fully;
never again will I make you
an object of scorn to the nations.

"I will drive the northern horde far from you,
pushing it into a parched and barren land;
its eastern ranks will drown in the Dead Sea
and its western ranks in the Mediterranean Sea...."

Be glad, people of Zion,
rejoice in the L*ORD* *your God,*
for he has given you the autumn rains
because he is faithful.
He sends you abundant showers,
both autumn and spring rains, as before.
The threshing floors will be filled with grain;
the vats will overflow with new wine and oil.

"I will repay you for the years the locusts have eaten—
the great locust and the young locust,
the other locusts and the locust swarm—
my great army that I sent among you....

Then you will know that I am in Israel,
that I am the L*ORD* *your God,*
and that there is no other."

JOEL 2:18–27

"I will repay you for the years the locusts have eaten—
the great locust and the young locust,
the other locusts and the locust swarm—
my great army that I sent among you."
JOEL 2:25

The beauty of the black lacy design against the pastel purple and orange background grabbed my attention. The intricacy of the fragile pattern led me to assume that it had been created by a skilled artist. As I looked more closely at the photo, however, I saw the artist admiring his work from a corner of the photo. The "artist" was a worm, and its work of art was a partially eaten leaf.

What made the image beautiful was not the destruction of the leaf but the light glowing through the holes. As I gazed at the photo, I began thinking about lives that have been eaten by the "worms" of sin. The effects are ravaging. Sin eats away at us as we suffer the consequences of our own bad choices or those of others. We are all its victims.

But the photo also reminded me of the hope we have in God. Through the prophet Joel, God said to Israel, "I will repay you for the years that the locusts have eaten" (Joel 2:25). And from Isaiah we learn that the Lord appointed him to "provide for those who grieve in Zion—to bestow on them beauty instead of ashes" (Isaiah 61:3).

Satan does everything he can to make us ugly, but the Light of the World can restore us and make us beautiful—despite Satan's best efforts.

Sins are like weeds in a garden;
we must pull them out or they will take over.

Keep your lives free from the love of money and be content with what you have, because God has said,

> *"Never will I leave you;*
> *never will I forsake you."*

So we say with confidence,

> *"The Lord is my helper; I will not be afraid.*
> *What can mere mortals do to me?"*

Remember your leaders, who spoke the word of God to you. Consider the outcome of their way of life and imitate their faith. Jesus Christ is the same yesterday and today and forever.

Do not be carried away by all kinds of strange teachings. It is good for our hearts to be strengthened by grace, not by eating ceremonial foods, which is of no benefit to those who do so. We have an altar from which those who minister at the tabernacle have no right to eat.

The high priest carries the blood of animals into the Most Holy Place as a sin offering, but the bodies are burned outside the camp. And so Jesus also suffered outside the city gate to make the people holy through his own blood. Let us, then, go to him outside the camp, bearing the disgrace he bore. For here we do not have an enduring city, but we are looking for the city that is to come.

Through Jesus, therefore, let us continually offer to God a sacrifice of praise—the fruit of lips that openly profess his name. And do not forget to do good and to share with others, for with such sacrifices God is pleased.

HEBREWS 13:5–16

You shall not covet your neighbor's house.
You shall not covet your neighbor's wife,
or his male or female servant.
EXODUS 20:17

The bird feeder attached to my office window is just beyond the reach of the squirrels. But one squirrel has made it his mission to get the seeds meant for the birds. Having seen his tiny neighbors nibbling noisily from the abundant supply, the squirrel is fixated on enjoying the same pleasure. He has tried coming at the feeder from every direction—but without success. He clawed his way up the wooden window casing to within inches of the feeder but slid down the slippery glass. He climbed the thin branches of the forsythia bush. Then he reached so far that he fell to the ground.

The squirrel's tireless attempts to get what isn't meant to be his calls to mind a man and woman who reached for food that wasn't meant to be theirs. They too suffered a fall—a fall so severe that it hurt the whole human race. Because they were disobedient and helped themselves to food that God told them not to eat, He put them where they could no longer reach it. As a result of their disobedience, they and their descendants must now work hard to get what He originally had given as a gift—food (see Genesis 2–3).

May our desire to have what God has kept from us not keep us from enjoying what He has given to us (Hebrews 13:5).

Godliness with contentment is great gain.
—1 TIMOTHY 6:6

Remember this: Whoever sows sparingly will also reap sparingly, and whoever sows generously will also reap generously. Each of you should give what you have decided in your heart to give, not reluctantly or under compulsion, for God loves a cheerful giver. And God is able to bless you abundantly, so that in all things at all times, having all that you need, you will abound in every good work. As it is written:

> *"They have freely scattered their gifts to the poor;*
> *their righteousness endures forever."*

Now he who supplies seed to the sower and bread for food will also supply and increase your store of seed and will enlarge the harvest of your righteousness. You will be enriched in every way so that you can be generous on every occasion, and through us your generosity will result in thanksgiving to God.

This service that you perform is not only supplying the needs of the Lord's people but is also overflowing in many expressions of thanks to God. Because of the service by which you have proved yourselves, others will praise God for the obedience that accompanies your confession of the gospel of Christ, and for your generosity in sharing with them and with everyone else. And in their prayers for you their hearts will go out to you, because of the surpassing grace God has given you. Thanks be to God for his indescribable gift!

2 CORINTHIANS 9:6–15

And God is able to bless you abundantly,
so that in all things at all times, having all that you need,
you will abound in every good work.
2 CORINTHIANS 9:8

Every year when I put out the hummingbird feeder, the busy little birds start battling for position. Even though there are four places at the "table," the birds fight for whatever place one of their neighbors is using. The source of food at each place is the same—a reservoir of syrup in the bottom of the feeder. Knowing that all the feeding stations are equal, I shake my head at their greediness.

But then I wonder, *Why is it so much easier to see the greed of the birds than it is to see my own?* I often want the place at "God's table" that someone else has, even though I know all good things come from the same source—God—and that His supply will never run out. Since God can prepare a table for us even in the presence of our enemies (Psalm 23:5), why be concerned that someone else might have the station in life that we want?

The Lord is able to give us "all sufficiency in all things" so that we will "abound in every good work" (2 Corinthians 9:8). When we recognize the importance of our work as ministers of the grace of God (1 Peter 4:10), we'll stop fighting to take over someone else's position and be grateful for the place God has given us to serve others on His behalf.

Resentment comes from looking at others;
contentment comes from looking at God.

Since, then, you have been raised with Christ, set your hearts on things above, where Christ is, seated at the right hand of God. Set your minds on things above, not on earthly things. For you died, and your life is now hidden with Christ in God. When Christ, who is your life, appears, then you also will appear with him in glory.

Put to death, therefore, whatever belongs to your earthly nature: sexual immorality, impurity, lust, evil desires and greed, which is idolatry. Because of these, the wrath of God is coming. You used to walk in these ways, in the life you once lived. But now you must also rid yourselves of all such things as these: anger, rage, malice, slander, and filthy language from your lips. Do not lie to each other, since you have taken off your old self with its practices and have put on the new self, which is being renewed in knowledge in the image of its Creator. Here there is no Gentile or Jew, circumcised or uncircumcised, barbarian, Scythian, slave or free, but Christ is all, and is in all.

Therefore, as God's chosen people, holy and dearly loved, clothe yourselves with compassion, kindness, humility, gentleness and patience. Bear with each other and forgive one another if any of you has a grievance against someone. Forgive as the Lord forgave you.

COLOSSIANS 3:1–13

Since, then, you have been raised with Christ,
set your hearts on things above, where Christ is,
seated at the right hand of God.
COLOSSIANS 3:1

Stepping outside and gazing heavenward on a star-studded evening always helps to soothe my soul after a trouble-filled day. When I peer into the night sky, I forget, at least for a moment, the cares of life on earth.

Ancient Israel's prolific songwriter wrote a poem thousands of years ago that still rings true: "When I consider your heavens, the work of your fingers, the moon and the stars, which you have set in place, what is mankind that you are mindful of them, human beings that you care for them?" (Psalm 8:3–4).

When we try to imagine the immensity of God's heavens, our problems indeed seem trivial. Yet God doesn't think so! With all the galaxies He has to attend to, God is mindful of us. And not only are we on His mind but He also cares for us.

No wonder the apostle Paul advised new believers to set their minds on things above (Colossians 3:2). In doing so, we raise our thoughts above the level of earthly disputes and focus instead on our loving, heavenly Father, who wants us to know Him, to know how to live peacefully with one another, and to know that we can live eternally with Him in a place even more beautiful than the heavens.

"The heavens declare the glory of God" (Psalm 19:1). Let's join creation in praise to Him.

Because God gives us everything,
we owe Him all our praise.

That night all the members of the community raised their voices and wept aloud. All the Israelites grumbled against Moses and Aaron, and the whole assembly said to them, "If only we had died in Egypt! Or in this wilderness! Why is the LORD bringing us to this land only to let us fall by the sword? Our wives and children will be taken as plunder. Wouldn't it be better for us to go back to Egypt?" And they said to each other, "We should choose a leader and go back to Egypt."

Then Moses and Aaron fell facedown in front of the whole Israelite assembly gathered there. Joshua son of Nun and Caleb son of Jephunneh, who were among those who had explored the land, tore their clothes and said to the entire Israelite assembly, "The land we passed through and explored is exceedingly good. If the LORD is pleased with us, he will lead us into that land, a land flowing with milk and honey, and will give it to us. Only do not rebel against the LORD. And do not be afraid of the people of the land, because we will devour them. Their protection is gone, but the LORD is with us. Do not be afraid of them."

But the whole assembly talked about stoning them. Then the glory of the LORD appeared at the tent of meeting to all the Israelites.

NUMBERS 14:1–10

If the LORD is pleased with us,
he will lead us into that land,
a land flowing with milk and honey,
and will give it to us.
NUMBERS 14:8

Eugene Cussons rescues chimpanzees. Orphaned by people in the business of bush-meat trade and taken from the jungle as infants, many of the chimps have lived their entire lives confined in a space smaller than a prison cell. When Cussons arrives to take them to the game reserve he calls "Chimp Eden," he often finds them hostile and untrusting.

"These chimps don't realize that I am one of the good guys," Cussons says. When he tries to put them into a smaller crate for the trip to their new home, they put up quite a fight. "They don't know that I'm going to take them back to Chimp Eden and give them a life so much better."

On a much grander scale, God's offer to liberate us from the slavery of sin is often met with resistance. When He rescued the children of Israel from Egypt, God took them through difficult places that caused them to doubt His good intentions. "Wouldn't it be better for us to go back to Egypt?" they cried (Numbers 14:3).

On our journey of faith, there are times when the "freedom" of sin that we left behind is more appealing than the restrictions of faith that lie ahead. We must trust the protective boundaries found in God's Word as the only way to get to the place of ultimate freedom.

Obedience to God is the key to freedom.

One day when Job's sons and daughters were feasting and drinking wine at the oldest brother's house, a messenger came to Job and said, "The oxen were plowing and the donkeys were grazing nearby, and the Sabeans attacked and made off with them. They put the servants to the sword, and I am the only one who has escaped to tell you!"

While he was still speaking, another messenger came and said, "The fire of God fell from the heavens and burned up the sheep and the servants, and I am the only one who has escaped to tell you!"

While he was still speaking, another messenger came and said, "The Chaldeans formed three raiding parties and swept down on your camels and made off with them. They put the servants to the sword, and I am the only one who has escaped to tell you!"

While he was still speaking, yet another messenger came and said, "Your sons and daughters were feasting and drinking wine at the oldest brother's house, when suddenly a mighty wind swept in from the desert and struck the four corners of the house. It collapsed on them and they are dead, and I am the only one who has escaped to tell you!"

At this, Job got up and tore his robe and shaved his head. Then he fell to the ground in worship and said:

> *"Naked I came from my mother's womb,*
> *and naked I will depart.*
> *The LORD gave and the LORD has taken away;*
> *may the name of the LORD be praised."*

In all this, Job did not sin by charging God with wrongdoing.

JOB 1:13–22

Indeed, we felt we had received the sentence of death.
But this happened that we might not rely
on ourselves but on God, who raises the dead.
2 CORINTHIANS 1:9

The geological features at Yellowstone National Park fascinate me. But when I walk among the geysers, I'm aware of how close I am to danger. I am walking atop one of the largest, most active volcanoes in the world.

When I read the book of Job, I feel as if I'm walking through Yellowstone on a day when the volcano erupts, exploding the earth's fragile crust and bringing disaster.

Like tourists at Yellowstone, Job was enjoying life. He was unaware that only a hedge separated him from disaster (Job 1:9–10). When God removed that hedge and allowed Satan to test Job, his life exploded (vv. 13–19).

Many believers live in circumstances where it seems as if God, for some reason, has removed His hedge of protection. Others, also for reasons unknown, live in relative calm, seemingly unaware of their fragile existence. Like Job's friends, they assume that nothing bad will happen unless they do something to deserve it.

As we learn from Job, however, God sometimes allows bad things to happen to good people. Although disaster can strike at any moment, nothing has the power to destroy those who trust Christ (2 Corinthians 4:9). No disaster can separate us from God's love.

God's love still stand
when all else has fallen.

But thanks be to God, who always leads us as captives in Christ's triumphal procession and uses us to spread the aroma of the knowledge of him everywhere. For we are to God the pleasing aroma of Christ among those who are being saved and those who are perishing. To the one we are an aroma that brings death; to the other, an aroma that brings life. And who is equal to such a task? Unlike so many, we do not peddle the word of God for profit. On the contrary, in Christ we speak before God with sincerity, as those sent from God.

2 CORINTHIANS 2:14–17

But thanks be to God, who always leads us as captives
in Christ's triumphal procession and uses us to
spread the aroma of the knowledge of him everywhere.
2 CORINTHIANS 2:14

You can't see it, hear it, or touch it, but scent is powerful. The smell of things like crayons, petunias, and colognes evoke memories that transport me to the past and bring to mind people and places I might not otherwise recall.

Some celebrities have fragrances named after them. Fans can identify with an actress or singer by dabbing on the scent bearing her name. Along those lines, *Ladies Home Journal* published a quiz to help readers determine the perfect fragrance for them. The idea is that every woman, to be memorable, should have a specific scent associated with her.

The idea of a signature scent is not new. God introduced it as part of worship. In the tabernacle, a certain scent was to be associated with the Lord (Exodus 30:34–35). The people were forbidden to use this fragrance for anything but worship (vv. 37–38).

This idea continues under the new covenant—but with a stunning difference. Instead of using incense to make people think of Him, God uses Christians as His "signature scent" to the world (2 Corinthians 2:14–15). The fact that God identifies himself with us in such a powerful way is a truly humbling thought. It causes me to ask, "What do people think about God as a result of being around me?"

A life lived for God
is a pleasing aroma.

One day, after Moses had grown up, he went out to where his own people were and watched them at their hard labor. He saw an Egyptian beating a Hebrew, one of his own people. Looking this way and that and seeing no one, he killed the Egyptian and hid him in the sand. The next day he went out and saw two Hebrews fighting. He asked the one in the wrong, "Why are you hitting your fellow Hebrew?"

The man said, "Who made you ruler and judge over us? Are you thinking of killing me as you killed the Egyptian?" Then Moses was afraid and thought, "What I did must have become known."

When Pharaoh heard of this, he tried to kill Moses, but Moses fled from Pharaoh and went to live in Midian, where he sat down by a well. Now a priest of Midian had seven daughters, and they came to draw water and fill the troughs to water their father's flock. Some shepherds came along and drove them away, but Moses got up and came to their rescue and watered their flock.

When the girls returned to Reuel their father, he asked them, "Why have you returned so early today?"

They answered, "An Egyptian rescued us from the shepherds. He even drew water for us and watered the flock."

"And where is he?" Reuel asked his daughters. "Why did you leave him? Invite him to have something to eat."

Moses agreed to stay with the man, who gave his daughter Zipporah to Moses in marriage. Zipporah gave birth to a son, and Moses named him Gershom, saying, "I have become a foreigner in a foreign land."

EXODUS 2:11–22

There is a time for everything,
and a season for every activity
under the heavens.
ECCLESIASTES 3:1

Where I live, this is the time of year when plants defy death by remaining underground until it is safe to come out again. Before the snow comes and the ground freezes, they let go of their beautiful blooms and retreat to a place where they can rest and save energy for the next growing season. Contrary to the way it looks, they are not dead; they are dormant. When the snow melts and the ground thaws, they will again lift their heads toward heaven, greeting their Creator with brilliant colors and sweet fragrances.

The seasons of life require that we sometimes enter a period of dormancy. We are not dead, but we may feel we've become invisible. During such times we may feel useless, and we may wonder whether God will ever use us again. But periods like this are for our protection and preparation. When the time is right and the conditions are safe, God will call us once again to service and worship.

Moses experienced a period of time like this. After killing an Egyptian who harmed a fellow Hebrew, Moses had to flee for his life to the distant land of the Midianites (Exodus 2:11–22). There, God protected him and prepared him for the biggest assignment of his life (3:10).

So be encouraged. We are never invisible to God.

No one is invisible to God.

Even so the body is not made up of one part but of many.

Now if the foot should say, "Because I am not a hand, I do not belong to the body," it would not for that reason stop being part of the body. And if the ear should say, "Because I am not an eye, I do not belong to the body," it would not for that reason stop being part of the body. If the whole body were an eye, where would the sense of hearing be? If the whole body were an ear, where would the sense of smell be? But in fact God has placed the parts in the body, every one of them, just as he wanted them to be. If they were all one part, where would the body be? As it is, there are many parts, but one body.

The eye cannot say to the hand, "I don't need you!" And the head cannot say to the feet, "I don't need you!" On the contrary, those parts of the body that seem to be weaker are indispensable, and the parts that we think are less honorable we treat with special honor. And the parts that are unpresentable are treated with special modesty, while our presentable parts need no special treatment. But God has put the body together, giving greater honor to the parts that lacked it, so that there should be no division in the body, but that its parts should have equal concern for each other. If one part suffers, every part suffers with it; if one part is honored, every part rejoices with it.

1 CORINTHIANS 12:14–26

There should be no division in the body, but ...
its parts should have equal concern for each other.
1 CORINTHIANS 12:25

After our plane landed on the gravel airstrip, Jay and I climbed out and entered the world of Masai Mara in Kenya. A Masai tribesman named Sammy met us and loaded our baggage into a Land Rover. Then we headed toward the camp where we would spend the next two days.

Stopping so we could watch the zebras and wildebeests migrating from Masai Mara to the Serengeti, Sammy explained that the two massive herds travel together because the zebras have good eyesight but a poor sense of smell, and the wildebeests have bad eyesight but a good sense of smell. By traveling together, both are less vulnerable to predators. This was our first lesson from God's revelation in creation, which Kenya has in abundance.

Just as God makes animals with different strengths and weaknesses, He makes people the same way. God made us to be dependent not only on Him but also on one another. The apostle Paul elaborated on this idea in his letter to the church in Corinth. As members of the body of Christ, we all have different gifts and abilities (1 Corinthians 12:12–31).

The church is healthy only when we work together, look out for each other, and use our strengths to benefit one another.

We can go a lot further together
than we can alone.

PART 5

Blessings and Burdens;
Challenges and Hope

Now Naaman was commander of the army of the king of Aram.... He was a valiant soldier, but he had leprosy.

Now bands of raiders from Aram had gone out and had taken captive a young girl from Israel, and she served Naaman's wife. She said to her mistress, "If only my master would see the prophet who is in Samaria! He would cure him of his leprosy."

Naaman went to his master and told him what the girl from Israel had said. "By all means, go," the king of Aram replied. "I will send a letter to the king of Israel." So Naaman left, taking with him ten talents of silver, six thousand shekels of gold and ten sets of clothing. The letter that he took to the king of Israel read: "With this letter I am sending my servant Naaman to you so that you may cure him of his leprosy."

As soon as the king of Israel read the letter, he tore his robes and said, "Am I God? Can I kill and bring back to life? Why does this fellow send someone to me to be cured of his leprosy? See how he is trying to pick a quarrel with me!"

When Elisha the man of God heard that the king of Israel had torn his robes, he sent him this message: "Why have you torn your robes? Have the man come to me and he will know that there is a prophet in Israel." So Naaman went with his horses and chariots and stopped at the door of Elisha's house. Elisha sent a messenger to say to him, "Go, wash yourself seven times in the Jordan, and your flesh will be restored and you will be cleansed."

But Naaman went away angry and said, "I thought that he would surely come out to me and stand and call on the name of the LORD his God, wave his hand over the spot and cure me of my leprosy...." So he turned and went off in a rage.

Naaman's servants went to him and said, "My father, if the prophet had told you to do some great thing, would you not have done it? How much more, then, when he tells you, 'Wash and be cleansed'!" So he went down and dipped himself in the Jordan seven times, as the man of God had told him, and his flesh was restored....

Then Naaman and all his attendants went back to the man of God. He stood before him and said, "Now I know that there is no God in all the world except in Israel. So please accept a gift from your servant."

2 KINGS 5:1–15

Naaman and all his attendants went back to the man of God. He stood before him and said, "Now I know that there is no God in all the world except in Israel."
2 KINGS 5:15

When I rear-ended a truck with my nearly new car, positive thoughts did not immediately come to mind. I was thinking primarily of the cost, the inconvenience, and the injury to my ego. But I did find some hope in this thought, which I often share with other writers: "In every bad experience, there's a good illustration."

Finding the good can be a challenge, but Scripture confirms that God uses bad circumstances for good purposes.

In 2 Kings 5, we find two people who had bad things happen to them. First is a young girl from Israel who was taken captive by the Syrian army. Second is Naaman, the commander of the army, who had leprosy. Even though the girl had good reason to desire bad things for her captors, she offered help instead. Israel's prophet Elisha, she said, could heal Naaman. Eager to be cured, Naaman went to Israel. However, he was reluctant to follow Elisha's humiliating directions. When he finally did, he was healed, which caused him to proclaim that Israel's God is the only God (v. 15).

God used two bad things—a kidnapping and a deadly disease—to change Israel's enemy into a friend. Even when we don't know why something bad happened, we know that God has the power to use it for good.

**God is the master
of turning burdens into blessings.**

"On one of these journeys I was going to Damascus with the authority and commission of the chief priests. About noon, King Agrippa, as I was on the road, I saw a light from heaven, brighter than the sun, blazing around me and my companions. We all fell to the ground, and I heard a voice saying to me in Aramaic, 'Saul, Saul, why do you persecute me? It is hard for you to kick against the goads.'

"Then I asked, 'Who are you, Lord?'

"'I am Jesus, whom you are persecuting,' the Lord replied. 'Now get up and stand on your feet. I have appeared to you to appoint you as a servant and as a witness of what you have seen and will see of me. I will rescue you from your own people and from the Gentiles. I am sending you to them to open their eyes and turn them from darkness to light, and from the power of Satan to God, so that they may receive forgiveness of sins and a place among those who are sanctified by faith in me.'

"So then, King Agrippa, I was not disobedient to the vision from heaven. First to those in Damascus, then to those in Jerusalem and in all Judea, and then to the Gentiles, I preached that they should repent and turn to God and demonstrate their repentance by their deeds. That is why some Jews seized me in the temple courts and tried to kill me. But God has helped me to this very day; so I stand here and testify to small and great alike. I am saying nothing beyond what the prophets and Moses said would happen—that the Messiah would suffer and, as the first to rise from the dead, would bring the message of light to his own people and to the Gentiles."

ACTS 26:12–23

*I preach that they should repent and turn to God
and demonstrate their repentance by their deeds.*
ACTS 26:20

One of my favorite *Peanuts* comic strips features Charlie Brown saying to Snoopy, "I hear you're writing a book on theology. I hope you have a good title." Snoopy responds, "I have the perfect title: *Has It Ever Occurred To You That You Might Be Wrong?*"

Snoopy's title reminds us that our understanding of God and what He requires of us is sometimes twisted. Because our wrong beliefs lead to wrong behavior, we need to "repent and turn to God and demonstrate their repentance by their deeds" (Acts 26:20).

The Greek word translated "repent" is *metanoeo*, which means, "change your mind." As Paul indicated, *repentance* does not mean just nodding in polite agreement with God and continuing the same way we were going. When we turn our thoughts toward God—when we truly agree with Him about what is right—our behavior will follow. Like a car, we go in the direction we are pointed. So, when we truly turn our minds and hearts toward God, our actions change accordingly.

Instead of going happily along, assuming that our choices are right, we need to regularly stop and ask ourselves Snoopy's question. As Paul taught, it is only when we are willing to admit being wrong that we can be certain of being right with God.

**Either we conform our desires to the truth
or we conform the truth to our desires.**
—OS GUINNESS

When they came to Geliloth near the Jordan in the land of Canaan, the Reubenites, the Gadites and the half-tribe of Manasseh built an imposing altar there by the Jordan. And when the Israelites heard that they had built the altar on the border of Canaan at Geliloth near the Jordan on the Israelite side, the whole assembly of Israel gathered at Shiloh to go to war against them.

So the Israelites sent Phinehas son of Eleazar, the priest, to the land of Gilead—to Reuben, Gad and the half-tribe of Manasseh. With him they sent ten of the chief men, one from each of the tribes of Israel, each the head of a family division among the Israelite clans.

When they went to Gilead—to Reuben, Gad and the half-tribe of Manasseh—they said to them: "The whole assembly of the LORD *says: 'How could you break faith with the God of Israel like this? How could you turn away from the* LORD *and build yourselves an altar in rebellion against him now?...*

Then Reuben, Gad and the half-tribe of Manasseh replied to the heads of the clans of Israel: "The Mighty One, God, the LORD! *The Mighty One, God, the* LORD! *He knows! And let Israel know!...*

"That is why we said, 'Let us get ready and build an altar— but not for burnt offerings or sacrifices.' On the contrary, it is to be a witness between us and you and the generations that follow, that we will worship the LORD *at his sanctuary with our burnt offerings, sacrifices and fellowship offerings...."*

When Phinehas the priest and the leaders of the community— the heads of the clans of the Israelites—heard what Reuben, Gad and Manasseh had to say, they were pleased. And Phinehas son of Eleazar, the priest, said to Reuben, Gad and Manasseh, "Today we know that the LORD *is with us, because you have not been unfaithful to the* LORD *in this matter. Now you have rescued the Israelites from the* LORD's *hand."*

JOSHUA 22:10–31

Do not be quickly provoked in your spirit,
for anger resides in the lap of fools.
ECCLESIASTES 7:9

The e-mail contained nothing but Bible verses, and it came from someone I didn't know very well at a time when there was disagreement among members of a church committee I was on. I assumed that the verses were aimed at me in an accusing way, and I was angry that someone who didn't know all the issues involved would use Scripture to attack me.

Before I could retaliate, my husband, Jay, suggested I give her the benefit of the doubt instead of assuming the worst. "Perhaps there's an innocent explanation," he said. I couldn't imagine what it would be, but I followed his advice and called. "Thank you so much for calling," she said. "My computer has a virus and it spewed out e-mails using pieces of our Sunday school lesson to random people in my address book." Gulp. I'm thankful that God used Jay to keep me from creating a problem where none existed.

By jumping to a conclusion that was logical but untrue, I came dangerously close to unnecessary conflict. The Israelites did the same thing. They were ready to go to war because they wrongly assumed that the altar built by their brothers was a sign of rebellion against God (Joshua 22:9–34). To avoid making wrong judgments, we must be careful to get the facts right.

To avoid an embarrassing fall,
don't jump to a wrong conclusion.

Praise the LORD.

Blessed are those who fear the LORD,
who find great delight in his commands.

Their children will be mighty in the land;
the generation of the upright will be blessed.
Wealth and riches are in their houses,
and their righteousness endures forever.
Even in darkness light dawns for the upright,
for those who are gracious and compassionate and righteous.
Good will come to those who are generous and lend freely,
who conduct their affairs with justice.

Surely the righteous will never be shaken;
they will be remembered forever.
They will have no fear of bad news;
their hearts are steadfast, trusting in the LORD.
Their hearts are secure, they will have no fear;
in the end they will look in triumph on their foes.
They have freely scattered their gifts to the poor,
their righteousness endures forever;
their horn will be lifted high in honor.

The wicked will see and be vexed,
they will gnash their teeth and waste away;
the longings of the wicked will come to nothing.

PSALM 112

Praise the LORD.
Blessed are those who fear the LORD,
who find great delight in his commands.
PSALM 112:1

I have a friend who's trying to find his way through the fog of doubt. While he still believes that God is good, much of what he's experiencing seems to contradict that. He's questioning the value of virtue because he sees another person's vice go unpunished. Although he knows that he ought to enjoy his walk with God, right now it's more duty than delight.

I also have an acquaintance who seems to be trying to hold on to God with one hand while clutching her sins in the other. I recently learned that her fourth marriage lasted less than a week. After paying thousands of dollars for a wedding, she's going to have to spend thousands more to get out of the marriage.

To anyone questioning the value of walking with God, I would reply: Saying no to selfish choices and saying yes to God's commands may not be easy, but it's the only way to experience true and lasting joy. Psalm 112 declares that the person who respects God and wants to please Him will enjoy His favor (v. 1). That doesn't guarantee a trouble-free life, of course, but it does assure us that we can have peace even in the tough times (vv. 6–8).

We can delight in knowing God's blessing is on us, even when the road is not easy.

**The cost of obedience
is nothing compared to the cost
of disobedience.**

Therefore, since Christ suffered in his body, arm yourselves also with the same attitude, because whoever suffers in the body is done with sin. As a result, they do not live the rest of their earthly lives for evil human desires, but rather for the will of God. For you have spent enough time in the past doing what pagans choose to do—living in debauchery, lust, drunkenness, orgies, carousing and detestable idolatry. They are surprised that you do not join them in their reckless, wild living, and they heap abuse on you. But they will have to give account to him who is ready to judge the living and the dead. For this is the reason the gospel was preached even to those who are now dead, so that they might be judged according to human standards in regard to the body, but live according to God in regard to the spirit.

The end of all things is near. Therefore be alert and of sober mind so that you may pray. Above all, love each other deeply, because love covers over a multitude of sins. Offer hospitality to one another without grumbling. Each of you should use whatever gift you have received to serve others, as faithful stewards of God's grace in its various forms. If anyone speaks, they should do so as one who speaks the very words of God. If anyone serves, they should do so with the strength God provides, so that in all things God may be praised through Jesus Christ. To him be the glory and the power for ever and ever. Amen.

1 PETER 4:1–11

A person's wisdom yields patience;
it is to one's glory to overlook an offense.
PROVERBS 19:11

I have nicknamed our car "No Grace." Sunday mornings are the worst. I load the car with all the stuff I need for church, get myself in my seat, close the door, and Jay starts backing out of the garage. While I am still getting settled, the seat belt warning starts buzzing. "Please," I say to it, "all I need is another minute." The answer, apparently, is no, because it continues buzzing until I am buckled in.

This minor annoyance is a good reminder of what life would be like if indeed there were no grace. Each of us would immediately be called to account for every indiscretion. There would be no time for repentance or change of behavior. There would be no forgiveness. No mercy. No hope.

Living in this world sometimes feels like falling into a no-grace sinkhole. When minor flaws are blown up into major indiscretions or when people refuse to overlook the faults and offenses of others, we end up burdened by the weight of guilt that we were never meant to carry. God, in His grace, sent Jesus to carry the burden for us. Those who receive God's gift of grace have the privilege of offering it to others on Christ's behalf: "Above all, love each other deeply, because love covers over a multitude of sins" (1 Peter 4:8).

When we gratefully acknowledge
the grace we've received,
we joyfully give it to those in need.

Moses said to God, "Suppose I go to the Israelites and say to them, 'The God of your fathers has sent me to you,' and they ask me, 'What is his name?' Then what shall I tell them?"

God said to Moses, "I AM WHO I AM. This is what you are to say to the Israelites: 'I AM has sent me to you.'"

God also said to Moses, "Say to the Israelites, 'The LORD, the God of your fathers—the God of Abraham, the God of Isaac and the God of Jacob—has sent me to you.'

> "This is my name forever,
> the name you shall call me
> from generation to generation.

"Go, assemble the elders of Israel and say to them, 'The LORD, the God of your fathers—the God of Abraham, Isaac and Jacob—appeared to me and said: I have watched over you and have seen what has been done to you in Egypt. And I have promised to bring you up out of your misery in Egypt into the land of the Canaanites, Hittites, Amorites, Perizzites, Hivites and Jebusites—a land flowing with milk and honey.'

"The elders of Israel will listen to you. Then you and the elders are to go to the king of Egypt and say to him, 'The LORD, the God of the Hebrews, has met with us. Let us take a three-day journey into the wilderness to offer sacrifices to the LORD our God.' But I know that the king of Egypt will not let you go unless a mighty hand compels him. So I will stretch out my hand and strike the Egyptians with all the wonders that I will perform among them. After that, he will let you go."

EXODUS 3:13–22

God said to Moses, "I AM WHO I AM.
This is what you are to say to the Israelites:
'I AM has sent me to you.'"
EXODUS 3:14

Thirty-five hundred years ago, Moses asked God who He was and got a peculiar answer. God said, "This is what you are to say to the Israelites: 'I AM has sent me to you.' ... This is my name forever" (Exodus 3:14–15).

I have long wondered why God would call himself by such a name, but slowly I am learning its significance. A sentence needs only two things to be complete: a subject and a verb. So when God says His name is "I AM," it conveys the concept that He is complete in himself. He is subject and verb. He is everything we could possibly need.

Jesus put flesh on God's bare-boned answer to Moses's question, "Who are You?" Jesus left heaven to show us what it means to bear His Father's name. He told His disciples, "I am the way and the truth and the life" (John 14:6). He also said, "I am the bread of life" (6:48), "the light of the world" (8:12), "the good shepherd" (10:11), and "the resurrection and the life" (11:25). In Revelation, Jesus declared, "I am the Alpha and the Omega, the Beginning and the End, the First and the Last" (22:13). And He said, "Before Abraham was, I AM" (John 8:58).

If you're questioning who God is, take some time to get to know Jesus in the pages of His Word.

Jesus is the image of the invisible God.
—COLOSSIANS 1:15

In the eighteenth year of the reign of Jeroboam son of Nebat, Abijah became king of Judah, 2 and he reigned in Jerusalem three years. His mother's name was Maakah daughter of Abishalom.

He committed all the sins his father had done before him; his heart was not fully devoted to the Lord his God, as the heart of David his forefather had been.

Nevertheless, for David's sake the Lord his God gave him a lamp in Jerusalem by raising up a son to succeed him and by making Jerusalem strong. For David had done what was right in the eyes of the Lord and had not failed to keep any of the Lord's commands all the days of his life—except in the case of Uriah the Hittite.

Asa did what was right in the eyes of the Lord, as his father David had done.

1 KINGS 15:1–5, 11

For David had done what was right
in the eyes of the LORD and had not failed to keep
any of the LORD's commands all the days of his life.
1 KINGS 15:5

One of the problems writers face is the challenge of being honest about evil. When I write, I want the good guys to always be right. But even the best people have flaws. So to be credible, writers must be honest about the evil that lurks in good people.

One reason I believe the Bible is true is that the Author did not cover up the flaws of His chosen people. God was honest about the failures of those He hand-picked for leadership positions. He didn't excuse their bad behavior, minimize their failures, or look the other way. He reported it, judged it, measured out the consequences, and forgave it.

The most prominent example in Scripture is King David. Not only did he take another man's wife but he also took the man's life to cover up his adultery. Yet despite his despicable deeds, when he was confronted, David repented. He became the standard by which future kings of Israel were judged because his heart was "loyal to the LORD" (1 Kings 15:3 NKJV).

God knows the heart of everyone, and He is no respecter of persons. Although the truth of sin can be painful, when it's confessed and forgiven, it can be used to turn our hearts toward God.

You can't put your sins behind you
until you are willing to face them.

Now I am ready to visit you for the third time, and I will not be a burden to you, because what I want is not your possessions but you. After all, children should not have to save up for their parents, but parents for their children. So I will very gladly spend for you everything I have and expend myself as well. If I love you more, will you love me less? Be that as it may, I have not been a burden to you. Yet, crafty fellow that I am, I caught you by trickery! Did I exploit you through any of the men I sent to you? I urged Titus to go to you and I sent our brother with him. Titus did not exploit you, did he? Did we not walk in the same footsteps by the same Spirit?

Have you been thinking all along that we have been defending ourselves to you? We have been speaking in the sight of God as those in Christ; and everything we do, dear friends, is for your strengthening. For I am afraid that when I come I may not find you as I want you to be, and you may not find me as you want me to be. I fear that there may be discord, jealousy, fits of rage, selfish ambition, slander, gossip, arrogance and disorder. I am afraid that when I come again my God will humble me before you, and I will be grieved over many who have sinned earlier and have not repented of the impurity, sexual sin and debauchery in which they have indulged.

2 CORINTHIANS 12:14–21

*So I very gladly spend for you everything
I have and expend myself as well.
If I love you more, will you love me less?*
2 CORINTHIANS 12:15

Before my husband and I travel, we go to the bank and trade in our US dollars for the currency of the country we'll be visiting. We do this so we can pay for expenses while we're away from home.

When we become Christians, another kind of exchange takes place. Our lives are like currency that we convert from one medium to another. We trade our old life for a new one so we can begin "spending" ourselves in a different kingdom. Instead of spending ourselves for the causes of this world, we are able to start spending ourselves for the cause of Christ.

The apostle Paul is a good example of this difference. After his dramatic conversion on the way to Damascus (Acts 9), he began spending his life in a dramatically different way. Instead of pursuing Christians to imprison and kill them, he began pursuing non-Christians to convert them. Then he spent the rest of his life for their welfare. He wrote to the church at Corinth, "I will very gladly spend for you everything I have and expend myself as well" (2 Corinthians 12:15). Everything he did was for the edification of his spiritual children (vv. 14, 19).

Conversion is far more than just changing our final destination. It's changing the way we spend each day of our lives.

**Conversion takes only a moment—
transformation takes a lifetime.**

So when we could stand it no longer, we thought it best to be left by ourselves in Athens. We sent Timothy, who is our brother and co-worker in God's service in spreading the gospel of Christ, to strengthen and encourage you in your faith, 3 so that no one would be unsettled by these trials. For you know quite well that we are destined for them. In fact, when we were with you, we kept telling you that we would be persecuted. And it turned out that way, as you well know. For this reason, when I could stand it no longer, I sent to find out about your faith. I was afraid that in some way the tempter had tempted you and that our labors might have been in vain.

But Timothy has just now come to us from you and has brought good news about your faith and love. He has told us that you always have pleasant memories of us and that you long to see us, just as we also long to see you. Therefore, brothers and sisters, in all our distress and persecution we were encouraged about you because of your faith. For now we really live, since you are standing firm in the Lord. How can we thank God enough for you in return for all the joy we have in the presence of our God because of you? Night and day we pray most earnestly that we may see you again and supply what is lacking in your faith.

Now may our God and Father himself and our Lord Jesus clear the way for us to come to you. May the Lord make your love increase and overflow for each other and for everyone else, just as ours does for you. May he strengthen your hearts so that you will be blameless and holy in the presence of our God and Father when our Lord Jesus comes with all his holy ones.

1 THESSALONIANS 3

So that no one would be unsettled by these trials.
For you know quite well that we are destined for them.
1 THESSALONIANS 3:3

Are parents trying too hard to make their kids happy? And is that having the opposite effect? These questions introduce an interview with Lori Gottlieb, author of an article on the subject of unhappy young adults. Her conclusion: Yes. Parents who refuse to let their children experience failure or sadness give them a false view of the world and do not prepare them for the harsh realities of adult life. They're left feeling empty and anxious.

Some Christians expect that the Lord will be the kind of parent who protects them from all sorrow and disappointment. But that's not the kind of Father He is. He lovingly allows His children to go through suffering (Isaiah 43:2; 1 Thessalonians 3:3).

When we start with the mistaken belief that it's an easy life that will make us truly happy, we become weary trying to live out our faulty belief. But when we face the truth that life is difficult, we can invest our lives in the pursuit of a good and godly life instead. That kind of life strengthens us for the times when life is difficult.

God's goal is to make us holy, not just happy (1 Thessalonians 3:13). And when we are holy, we are more likely to be truly happy and content.

**A contented person has learned
to accept the bitter with the sweet.**

So the Pharisees and teachers of the law asked Jesus, "Why don't your disciples live according to the tradition of the elders instead of eating their food with defiled hands?"

He replied, "Isaiah was right when he prophesied about you hypocrites; as it is written:

" 'These people honor me with their lips,
but their hearts are far from me.
They worship me in vain;
their teachings are merely human rules.'

You have let go of the commands of God and are holding on to human traditions."

And he continued, "You have a fine way of setting aside the commands of God in order to observe your own traditions! For Moses said, 'Honor your father and mother,' and, 'Anyone who curses their father or mother is to be put to death.' But you say that if anyone declares that what might have been used to help their father or mother is Corban (that is, devoted to God)— then you no longer let them do anything for their father or mother. Thus you nullify the word of God by your tradition that you have handed down. And you do many things like that."

Again Jesus called the crowd to him and said, "Listen to me, everyone, and understand this. Nothing outside a person can defile them by going into them. Rather, it is what comes out of a person that defiles them."

MARK 7:5–15

*"These people honor me with their lips,
but their hearts are far from me."*
MARK 7:6

"Smile," Jay said to me as we drove to church. "You look so unhappy." I wasn't; I was just thinking, and I can't do two things at once. But to make him happy, I smiled. "Not like that," he said. "I mean a real smile."

His comment got me thinking even more intently. Is it reasonable to expect a real smile from someone who's being issued a command? A real smile comes from inside; it's an expression of the heart, not of the face.

We settle for phony smiles in photographs. We're happy when everyone cooperates at the photographer's studio, and we get at least one picture with everyone smiling. After all, we're creating an icon of happiness, so it doesn't have to be genuine.

But phoniness before God is unacceptable. Whether we're happy or sad or mad, honesty is essential. God doesn't want false expressions of worship any more than He wants false statements about people or circumstances (Mark 7:6).

Changing our facial expression is easier than changing our attitude, but true worship requires that all of our heart, soul, mind, and strength agree that God is worthy of praise. Even when our circumstances are sad, we can be grateful for God's mercy and compassion, which are worth more than the "lip service" of a phony smile.

**A song in the heart
puts a smile on the face.**

This is what the LORD *Almighty says:*

> *"Do not listen to what the prophets are prophesying*
> > *to you;*
> > *they fill you with false hopes.*
> *They speak visions from their own minds,*
> > *not from the mouth of the* LORD.
> *They keep saying to those who despise me,*
> > *'The* LORD *says: You will have peace.'*
> *And to all who follow the stubbornness of their hearts*
> > *they say, 'No harm will come to you.'*
> *But which of them has stood in the council of the* LORD
> > *to see or to hear his word?*
> > *Who has listened and heard his word?*
> *See, the storm of the* LORD
> > *will burst out in wrath,*
> *a whirlwind swirling down*
> > *on the heads of the wicked.*
> *The anger of the* LORD *will not turn back*
> > *until he fully accomplishes*
> > *the purposes of his heart....*

> *"Am I only a God nearby,"*
> > *declares the* LORD,
> > *"and not a God far away?"*

JEREMIAH 23:16–23

*"Woe to the shepherds who are destroying and
scattering the sheep of my pasture!" declares the LORD.*
JEREMIAH 23:1

In 1517, Martin Luther nailed his Ninety-Five Theses to the door of the castle church in Wittenberg. Luther became known as a reformer, and we remember his bold stand as a turning point in church history.

The fiery priest demonstrated great courage in expressing outrage at the church's practice of selling forgiveness through indulgences, which allowed the people to sin intentionally in exchange for money.

Luther's passion to stop these practices did not make him popular with the religious authorities of his day. In fact, his efforts resulted in a series of attempts to silence him.

Long before Luther, the prophet Jeremiah felt the power of God's Word in his heart "like a fire, a fire shut up in my bones. I am weary of holding it in; indeed, I cannot" (Jeremiah 20:9). Jeremiah and Luther refused to allow God's truth to be compromised.

Living for God is about grace and forgiveness, but it's also about boldly standing for the truth. Having God's Word in our heart doesn't always result in warm, pleasant feelings. Sometimes His truth becomes a blazing fire that causes us to challenge corruption—even though we may be attacked for it.

**It's better to declare the truth and be rejected
than to withhold it just to be accepted.**

Dear friends, this is now my second letter to you. I have written both of them as reminders to stimulate you to wholesome thinking. I want you to recall the words spoken in the past by the holy prophets and the command given by our Lord and Savior through your apostles.

Above all, you must understand that in the last days scoffers will come, scoffing and following their own evil desires. They will say, "Where is this 'coming' he promised? Ever since our ancestors died, everything goes on as it has since the beginning of creation." But they deliberately forget that long ago by God's word the heavens came into being and the earth was formed out of water and by water. By these waters also the world of that time was deluged and destroyed. By the same word the present heavens and earth are reserved for fire, being kept for the day of judgment and destruction of the ungodly.

But do not forget this one thing, dear friends: With the Lord a day is like a thousand years, and a thousand years are like a day. The Lord is not slow in keeping his promise, as some understand slowness. Instead he is patient with you, not wanting anyone to perish, but everyone to come to repentance.

2 PETER 3:1–9

The Lord is not slow in keeping his promise,
as some understand slowness.
Instead he is patient with you,
not wanting any to perish.
2 PETER 3:9

If there were a contest for most popular virtue, I suspect that "fast" would beat "best." Many parts of the world seem to be obsessed with speed. The "fast" craze, however, is getting us nowhere—fast.

"The time has come to challenge our obsession with doing everything more quickly," says Carl Honoré in his book *In Praise of Slowness.* "Speed is not always the best policy."

According to the Bible, he's right. Peter warned that in the last days people would doubt God because it seems He is slow in fulfilling His promise to return. Peter pointed out, however, that this seeming slowness is a good thing. God is actually demonstrating His patience by giving people more time to repent (2 Peter 3:9) and also being true to His character—as in patient or slow to anger (Exodus 34:6).

We too must be slow to become angry—and slow to speak (James 1:19). According to James, "quickness" is reserved for our ears. We're supposed to be "quick to listen." Think about how much trouble we could avoid if we learned to listen— really listen, not just stop talking—before we speak.

In our rush to meet goals and deadlines, let's remember to speed up our listening and to slow down our tempers and our tongues.

When you're tempted to lose patience with another, remember how patient God has been with you.

I saw in heaven another great and marvelous sign: seven angels with the seven last plagues—last, because with them God's wrath is completed. And I saw what looked like a sea of glass glowing with fire and, standing beside the sea, those who had been victorious over the beast and its image and over the number of its name. They held harps given them by God and sang the song of God's servant Moses and of the Lamb:

> *"Great and marvelous are your deeds,*
> *Lord God Almighty.*
> *Just and true are your ways,*
> *King of the nations.*
> *Who will not fear you, Lord,*
> *and bring glory to your name?*
> *For you alone are holy.*
> *All nations will come*
> *and worship before you,*
> *for your righteous acts have been revealed."*

After this I looked, and I saw in heaven the temple—that is, the tabernacle of the covenant law—and it was opened. Out of the temple came the seven angels with the seven plagues. They were dressed in clean, shining linen and wore golden sashes around their chests. Then one of the four living creatures gave to the seven angels seven golden bowls filled with the wrath of God, who lives for ever and ever. And the temple was filled with smoke from the glory of God and from his power, and no one could enter the temple until the seven plagues of the seven angels were completed.

REVELATION 15

Who will not fear you, Lord,
and bring glory to your name?
REVELATION 15:4

Some of the words normally used to describe the opening ceremony of the Summer Olympic Games are *awesome, breathtaking,* and *extravagant.* Speaking of the 2008 opener in Beijing, one commentator observed, "This shows what happens when you give an artist an unlimited budget."

When I heard this, I thought, *That's what God did at creation! He held nothing back.* The resulting universe is stunning in beauty, staggering in complexity, extravagant in all regards.

That 2008 Olympic ceremony was perfect in its precision; but if just one drummer or dancer had decided to alter the artist's vision, the whole ceremony would have been flawed.

That's what happened shortly after creation. Unlike the Olympic producer, God allowed free choice, and His work of art was marred by Adam and Eve's idea of a better way. In Isaiah's words, "Each of us has turned to our own way" (53:6).

God's solution to our waywardness was unimaginable: The Artist paid the price to recreate what we ruined. One day, there will be another opening ceremony, and everyone in heaven and on earth will bow at the name of Jesus (Philippians 2:10). And those from every nation who have accepted God's plan in Christ will worship together in the flawless New Jerusalem (Revelation 15:4).

We have all eternity to praise God—
begin today.

The vision concerning Judah and Jerusalem that Isaiah son of Amoz saw during the reigns of Uzziah, Jotham, Ahaz and Hezekiah, kings of Judah.

> *Hear me, you heavens! Listen, earth!*
>   *For the* LORD *has spoken:*
> *"I reared children and brought them up,*
>   *but they have rebelled against me.*
> *The ox knows its master,*
>   *the donkey its owner's manger,*
> *but Israel does not know,*
>   *my people do not understand."*
>
> *Woe to the sinful nation,*
>   *a people whose guilt is great,*
> *a brood of evildoers,*
>   *children given to corruption!*
> *They have forsaken the* LORD*;*
>   *they have spurned the Holy One of Israel*
>   *and turned their backs on him....*
>
> *"The multitude of your sacrifices—*
>   *what are they to me?" says the* LORD*....*
>
> *Stop bringing meaningless offerings!*
>   *Your incense is detestable to me....*
>
> *Wash and make yourselves clean.*
>   *Take your evil deeds out of my sight;*
>   *stop doing wrong.*

ISAIAH 1:1–16

Learn to do right; seek justice.
Defend the oppressed.
Take up the cause of the fatherless;
plead the case of the widow.
ISAIAH 1:17

After reading Isaiah 1, I thought of this riddle: What is heavy for God when it's empty for me?

Nothing is too hard for God to do, of course, but that doesn't mean that nothing is a burden to Him. In fact, one thing I sometimes take lightly is actually a heavy concern to God.

In the time of the prophet Isaiah, the Jewish people followed their religious celebrations to the letter. They showed up at the right time, sacrificed the right amount, and offered many prayers. But when they left the temple, it was as if they left God there.

Nearly 3,000 years later, not much has changed. Sometimes I think my responsibility to God begins and ends with going to church and giving an offering. But this attitude makes me more of a burden to God than a blessing. I'm not accomplishing the tasks that are important to Him—doing good, seeking justice, defending the fatherless, and pleading for widows (Isaiah 1:17).

God is not impressed with a full house at religious gatherings if the people come with empty hearts. God wants worshipers with hearts so full of love for Him that they overflow in good deeds for others.

Oh, are you still wondering what is heavy for God when it's empty for me? The answer is *worship*.

The heart filled with praise
brings pleasure to God.

So Bezalel, Oholiab and every skilled person to whom the LORD has given skill and ability to know how to carry out all the work of constructing the sanctuary are to do the work just as the LORD has commanded."

Then Moses summoned Bezalel and Oholiab and every skilled person to whom the LORD had given ability and who was willing to come and do the work. They received from Moses all the offerings the Israelites had brought to carry out the work of constructing the sanctuary. And the people continued to bring free-will offerings morning after morning. So all the skilled workers who were doing all the work on the sanctuary left what they were doing and said to Moses, "The people are bringing more than enough for doing the work the LORD commanded to be done."

Then Moses gave an order and they sent this word throughout the camp: "No man or woman is to make anything else as an offering for the sanctuary." And so the people were restrained from bringing more, because what they already had was more than enough to do all the work.

EXODUS 36:1–7

*All who are skilled among you are to come
and make everything the LORD has commanded.*
EXODUS 35:10

When my husband, Jay, and I decided to build a new house, we didn't recruit friends and family who enjoy working with power tools; instead we hired a skilled builder to create something both functional and beautiful.

Beauty in the church building, however, is not always a high priority. Some associate it with impracticality, so anything ornate or decorative is considered wasteful. But that wasn't God's attitude when He established a place of worship for the ancient Israelites. He didn't recruit just anybody to set up an ordinary tent. He appointed skilled craftsmen, Bezalel and Oholiab (Exodus 36:1), to decorate the tabernacle with finely woven tapestries and intricately designed ornaments (37:17–20).

I think the beauty was important then because it reminded the people of the worth of God in their worship. During the dry and dusty days of desert wanderings, they needed a reminder of God's majesty.

The beauty created by God's people in worship settings today can serve the same purpose. We offer God our best talents because He is worthy. Beauty also gives us a glimpse of heaven and whets our appetites for what God is preparing for our future.

Beauty reflects God.

Then David said, "The house of the LORD God is to be here, and also the altar of burnt offering for Israel...."

David said, "My son Solomon is young and inexperienced, and the house to be built for the LORD should be of great magnificence and fame and splendor in the sight of all the nations. Therefore I will make preparations for it." So David made extensive preparations before his death.

Then he called for his son Solomon and charged him to build a house for the LORD, the God of Israel....

"Now, my son, the LORD be with you, and may you have success and build the house of the LORD your God, as he said you would. May the LORD give you discretion and understanding when he puts you in command over Israel, so that you may keep the law of the LORD your God. Then you will have success if you are careful to observe the decrees and laws that the LORD gave Moses for Israel. Be strong and courageous. Do not be afraid or discouraged.

"I have taken great pains to provide for the temple of the LORD a hundred thousand talents of gold, a million talents of silver, quantities of bronze and iron too great to be weighed, and wood and stone. And you may add to them. You have many workers: stonecutters, masons and carpenters, as well as those skilled in every kind of work in gold and silver, bronze and iron—craftsmen beyond number. Now begin the work, and the LORD be with you."

Then David ordered all the leaders of Israel to help his son Solomon.

1 CHRONICLES 22

*David said, "My son Solomon is young
and inexperienced, and the house to be built for
the LORD should be of great magnificence and fame
and splendor in the sight of all the nations."*
1 CHRONICLES 22:5

We had rehearsed the song for several weeks, and it sounded good. But there was one tricky section we just couldn't get right. We were ready to call it good enough. Our choir director seemed to agree. He too was weary of rehearsing the same few measures over and over.

Finally he said, "We've worked hard on this. You're tired. I'm tired. We're running short on time. And 99 percent of the people won't know whether or not we sing it right." As we started to put away our music, he continued, "But we're going to sing it right for the 1 percent who know the difference." We groaned as we reopened our music to the rumpled page.

On Sunday morning when we sang it right, few people knew. But that didn't matter. What really mattered was that we were singing from our heart for an audience of One—One who deserves excellent praise.

King David wanted a house of "great magnificence" to be built for the Lord (1 Chronicles 22:5). So before he died, he made sure his son Solomon had everything he needed to build the temple—an abundance of gold, silver, bronze, iron, timber, stone, and skilled craftsmen (vv. 14–15).

Whatever we do, our audience of One deserves our very best.

**When we worship God,
only our best is good enough.**

David summoned all the officials of Israel to assemble at Jerusalem: the officers over the tribes, the commanders of the divisions in the service of the king, the commanders of thousands and commanders of hundreds, and the officials in charge of all the property and livestock belonging to the king and his sons, together with the palace officials, the warriors and all the brave fighting men.

King David rose to his feet and said: "Listen to me, my fellow Israelites, my people. I had it in my heart to build a house as a place of rest for the ark of the covenant of the LORD, *for the footstool of our God, and I made plans to build it. But God said to me, 'You are not to build a house for my Name, because you are a warrior and have shed blood.'*

"Yet the LORD, *the God of Israel, chose me from my whole family to be king over Israel forever. He chose Judah as leader, and from the tribe of Judah he chose my family, and from my father's sons he was pleased to make me king over all Israel. Of all my sons—and the* LORD *has given me many—he has chosen my son Solomon to sit on the throne of the kingdom of the* LORD *over Israel. He said to me: 'Solomon your son is the one who will build my house and my courts, for I have chosen him to be my son, and I will be his father. I will establish his kingdom forever if he is unswerving in carrying out my commands and laws, as is being done at this time.'*

"So now I charge you in the sight of all Israel and of the assembly of the LORD, *and in the hearing of our God: Be careful to follow all the commands of the* LORD *your God, that you may possess this good land and pass it on as an inheritance to your descendants forever."*

1 CHRONICLES 28:1–8

King David rose to his feet and said:
"... I had it in my heart to build a house as a place
of rest for the ark of the covenant of the LORD."
1 CHRONICLES 28:2

I poured my heart into worship ministries at church because I love helping people connect Sunday worship with personal, daily worship. I served on committees and as a chaplain for choir and orchestra; I wrote weekly prayers for the worship folder and daily prayer prompters for each day's Bible reading; I worked with our worship pastor to plan services. Then he resigned.

When the search committee was formed to find his replacement, I was not asked to be on it, and I let it be known that I felt used and unappreciated. I tried to argue myself out of my bad attitude, but with little success. Then, while working on the next week's worship folder, I was stopped in my tracks by words I had written a year earlier. As I typed the prayer prompter to go with 1 Chronicles 25–29, which includes the account of David's unfulfilled desire to build the temple, my own words convicted me: "Pray that we will not be resentful when God gives to someone else the task we were hoping to do."

I immediately called the chairman of the search committee to confess my bad attitude and to promise that I would support him in the difficult task ahead. And I continue to do that because the work belongs to God, not to me!

**Be faithful—
and leave the results to God.**

At mealtime Boaz said to [Ruth], "Come over here. Have some bread and dip it in the wine vinegar." When she sat down with the harvesters, he offered her some roasted grain. She ate all she wanted and had some left over. As she got up to glean, Boaz gave orders to his men, "Let her gather among the sheaves and don't reprimand her. Even pull out some stalks for her from the bundles and leave them for her to pick up, and don't rebuke her."

So Ruth gleaned in the field until evening. Then she threshed the barley she had gathered, and it amounted to about an ephah. She carried it back to town, and her mother-in-law saw how much she had gathered. Ruth also brought out and gave her what she had left over after she had eaten enough.

Her mother-in-law asked her, "Where did you glean today? Where did you work? Blessed be the man who took notice of you!" Then Ruth told her mother-in-law about the one at whose place she had been working. "The name of the man I worked with today is Boaz," she said.

"The LORD bless him!" Naomi said to her daughter-in-law. "He has not stopped showing his kindness to the living and the dead." She added, "That man is our close relative; he is one of our guardian-redeemers."

Then Ruth the Moabite said, "He even said to me, 'Stay with my workers until they finish harvesting all my grain.'"

Naomi said to Ruth her daughter-in-law, "It will be good for you, my daughter, to go with the women who work for him, because in someone else's field you might be harmed."

So Ruth stayed close to the women of Boaz.

RUTH 2:14–23

He will renew your life
and sustain you in your old age.
RUTH 4:15

Naomi and Ruth came together in less-than-ideal circumstances. To escape a famine in Israel, Naomi's family moved to Moab. While living there, her two sons married Moabite women: Orpah and Ruth. Then Naomi's husband and sons died. In that culture, women were dependent on men, which left the three widows in a predicament.

Word came to Naomi that the famine in Israel had ended, so she decided to make the long trek home. Orpah and Ruth started to go with her, but Naomi urged them to return home, saying, "The LORD's hand has turned against me!" (1:13).

Orpah went home, but Ruth continued, affirming her belief in Naomi's God despite Naomi's own fragile faith (1:15–18).

The story started in desperately unpleasant circumstances: famine, death, and despair (1:1–5). It changed direction due to undeserved kindnesses: Ruth to Naomi (1:16–17; 2:11–12) and Boaz to Ruth (2:13–14).

It involved unlikely people: two widows (an aging Jew and a young Gentile) and Boaz, the son of a prostitute (Joshua 2:1; Matthew 1:5).

It depended on unexplainable intervention: Ruth just so "happened" to glean in the field of Boaz (2:3).

And it ended in unimaginable blessing: a baby who would be in the lineage of the Messiah (4:16–17).

God makes miracles out of what seems insignificant: fragile faith, a little kindness, and ordinary people.

**In all the setbacks of your life as a believer,
God is plotting for your joy.**
—JOHN PIPER

"As the Father has loved me, so have I loved you. Now remain in my love. If you keep my commands, you will remain in my love, just as I have kept my Father's commands and remain in his love. I have told you this so that my joy may be in you and that your joy may be complete. My command is this: Love each other as I have loved you. Greater love has no one than this: to lay down one's life for one's friends. You are my friends if you do what I command. I no longer call you servants, because a servant does not know his master's business. Instead, I have called you friends, for everything that I learned from my Father I have made known to you. You did not choose me, but I chose you and appointed you so that you might go and bear fruit—fruit that will last—and so that whatever you ask in my name the Father will give you. This is my command: Love each other."

JOHN 15:9–17

I no longer call you servants,
because a servant does not know his master's business.
Instead, I have called you friends.
JOHN 15:15-16

Someone has defined friendship as "knowing the heart of another and sharing one's heart with another." We share our hearts with those we trust, and trust those who care about us. We confide in our friends because we have confidence that they will use the information to help us, not harm us. They in turn confide in us for the same reason.

We often refer to Jesus as our friend because we know that He wants what is best for us. We confide in Him because we trust Him. But have you ever considered that Jesus confides in His people?

Jesus began calling His disciples friends rather than servants because He had entrusted them with everything He had heard from His Father (John 15:15). Jesus trusted the disciples to use the information for the good of His Father's kingdom.

Although we know that Jesus is our friend, can we say that we are His friends? Do we listen to Him? Or do we only want Him to listen to us? Do we want to know what's on His heart? Or do we only want to tell Him what's on ours? To be a friend of Jesus, we need to listen to what He wants us to know and then use the information to bring others into friendship with Him.

Christ's friendship calls
for our faithfulness.

Then, at the evening sacrifice, I rose from my self-abasement, with my tunic and cloak torn, and fell on my knees with my hands spread out to the LORD my God and prayed:

"I am too ashamed and disgraced, my God, to lift up my face to you, because our sins are higher than our heads and our guilt has reached to the heavens. From the days of our ancestors until now, our guilt has been great. Because of our sins, we and our kings and our priests have been subjected to the sword and captivity, to pillage and humiliation at the hand of foreign kings, as it is today.

"But now, for a brief moment, the LORD our God has been gracious in leaving us a remnant and giving us a firm place in his sanctuary, and so our God gives light to our eyes and a little relief in our bondage. Though we are slaves, our God has not forsaken us in our bondage. He has shown us kindness in the sight of the kings of Persia: He has granted us new life to rebuild the house of our God and repair its ruins, and he has given us a wall of protection in Judah and Jerusalem."

EZRA 9:5–9

*At the present time
there is a remnant chosen by grace.*
ROMANS 11:5

The lone tree in the field across from my office remained a mystery. Acres of trees had been cut down so the farmer could grow corn. But one tree remained standing—its branches reaching up and spreading out. The mystery was solved when I learned that the tree was spared for a purpose. Long ago, farmers traditionally left one tree standing so they and their animals would have a cool place to rest when the hot summer sun was beating down.

At times we find that we alone have survived something, and we don't know why. Soldiers coming home from combat and patients who have survived a life-threatening illness struggle to know why they survived when others did not.

The Old Testament speaks of a remnant of Israelites God spared when the nation was sent into exile. The remnant preserved God's law and later rebuilt the temple (Ezra 9:9). The apostle Paul referred to himself as part of the remnant of God (Romans 11:1, 5). He was spared to become God's messenger to Gentiles (v. 13).

If we stand where others have fallen, it's to raise our hands to heaven in praise and to spread our arms as shade for the weary. The Lord enables us to be a tree of rest for others.

**Hope can be ignited
by a spark of encouragement.**

In my former book, Theophilus, I wrote about all that Jesus began to do and to teach until the day he was taken up to heaven, after giving instructions through the Holy Spirit to the apostles he had chosen. After his suffering, he presented himself to them and gave many convincing proofs that he was alive. He appeared to them over a period of forty days and spoke about the kingdom of God. On one occasion, while he was eating with them, he gave them this command: "Do not leave Jerusalem, but wait for the gift my Father promised, which you have heard me speak about. For John baptized with water, but in a few days you will be baptized with the Holy Spirit."

Then they gathered around him and asked him, "Lord, are you at this time going to restore the kingdom to Israel?"

He said to them: "It is not for you to know the times or dates the Father has set by his own authority. But you will receive power when the Holy Spirit comes on you; and you will be my witnesses in Jerusalem, and in all Judea and Samaria, and to the ends of the earth."

After he said this, he was taken up before their very eyes, and a cloud hid him from their sight.

They were looking intently up into the sky as he was going, when suddenly two men dressed in white stood beside them. "Men of Galilee," they said, "why do you stand here looking into the sky? This same Jesus, who has been taken from you into heaven, will come back in the same way you have seen him go into heaven."

ACTS 1:1–11

When the husband of my longtime friend and publishing colleague collapsed and later died, there was no doubt that life had slipped away from him. There were witnesses. The same was true when Jesus died. But three days later, Jesus was raised from the dead! We have no doubt that this is true because there were witnesses who later saw Him alive.

When we gathered for Dave's memorial service, we read familiar passages of Scripture that affirm our hope that he is now enjoying new life in heaven. But we claimed these promises by faith because none of us witnessed Dave go to heaven. There was, however, a witness who saw Jesus in heaven. Not long after witnesses saw Jesus ascend (Acts 1:9), Stephen saw the heavens open "and the Son of Man standing at the right hand of God" (7:56). One of the reasons we know that Jesus spoke the truth about going to prepare a place for us (John 14:2) is that He has been seen alive in heaven.

When a loved one goes ahead of us to heaven, we feel as if we're being pulled in the opposite direction—down into an abyss of sadness. Yet, because God kept His promise to raise Christ and take Him to heaven, we can trust Him to do the same for all who love and follow Him.

The promise of heaven
is our eternal hope.

The LORD is my shepherd, I lack nothing.
He makes me lie down in green pastures,
he leads me beside quiet water
he refreshes my soul.
He guides me along the right paths
for his name's sake.
Even though I walk
through the darkest valley,
I will fear no evil,
for you are with me;
your rod and your staff,
they comfort me.

You prepare a table before me
in the presence of my enemies.
You anoint my head with oil;
my cup overflows.
Surely your goodness and love will follow me
all the days of my life,
and I will dwell in the house of the LORD
forever.

PSALM 23

For you have been my hope, Sovereign LORD,
my confidence since my youth.
PSALM 71:5

The ancient road from Jerusalem to Jericho is a narrow, treacherous path along a deep gorge in the Judean wilderness. Its name is Wadi Kelt, but it's known as the valley of the shadow, for this is the location that inspired David's twenty-third Psalm. The place itself offers little reason to compose such a hopeful poem. The landscape is bleak, barren, and perilously steep. It's a good place for thieves but not for anyone else.

When David wrote, "Yea, though I walk through the valley of the shadow of death, I will fear no evil" (Psalm 23:4 NKJV), he was in a place where evil was an ever-present reality. Yet he refused to give in to fear. He wasn't expressing hope that God would abolish evil so that he could pass through safely; he was saying that the presence of God gave him the confidence to pass through difficult places without fear of being deserted by Him. In another psalm, David said that the Lord was his hope (71:5).

Many claim to have hope, but only those whose hope is Christ can claim it with certainty. Hope comes not from strength, intelligence, or favorable circumstances, but from the Lord. As Maker of heaven and earth, He alone has the right to promise hope and the power to keep the promise.

**Hope for the Christian is a certainty—
because its basis is Christ.**

Enjoy this book? Help us get the word out!

Share a link to the book or
mention it on social media

Write a review on your blog, on a retailer site,
or on our website (dhp.org)

Pick up another copy to share with someone

Recommend this book for your
church, book club, or small group

Follow Discovery House on
social media and join the discussion

Contact us to share your thoughts:

 @discoveryhouse   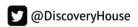 @DiscoveryHouse

Discovery House
P.O. Box 3566
Grand Rapids, MI 49501 USA

Phone: 1-800-653-8333
Email: books@dhp.org
Web: dhp.org